D1123878

A Cultural History of the United States

Through the Decades

The 1990s

A Cultural History of the United States

Through the Decades

The 1990s

Stuart A. Kallen

Lucent Books, Inc., San Diego, California

Library of Congress Cataloging-in-Publication Data

Kallen, Stuart A., 1955–
The 1990s / by Stuart A. Kallen.
p. cm.—(A cultural history of the United States through the decades)
Includes bibliographical references and index.
ISBN 1-56006-559-1 (alk. paper)
1. United States—History—1969– —Juvenile literature. 2. United States—Social conditions—1980– —Juvenile literature.
3. United States—Social life and customs—1971– —Juvenile literature. 4. Nineteen nineties—Juvenile literature. I. Title. II. Series.
E881.K355 1999
973.92—dc21 98-30359
CIP
AC

P.O. Box 289011, San Diego, California 92198-9011

Printed in the U.S.A.

Contents

A man in West Berlin swings a sledgehammer to help destroy the Berlin Wall on November 12, 1989. The destruction of the wall was one of the most visible signs of the end of the cold war.

Examining the Eighties

The 1990s should be known as the "wired decade" or the "interactive decade." Borders, boundaries, and distances dissolved as the Internet, cellular phones, fax machines, and pagers allowed people instant communications. For the first time since its invention, television *lost* viewers, many of them to the Internet. Hundreds of new choices were available allowing interactive participation in the worlds of politics, entertainment, and the arts.

Borders and boundaries also fell away for businesses. German cars were assembled in Alabama, American computers were built in Indonesia, and money flew across satellite phone lines as investors entered stock markets in Hong Kong, Russia, and elsewhere. It seemed as if restrictions on information dissolved as the world entered the twenty-first century.

The 1990s brought to culmination many of the communications trends of the 1980s, when personal computers first appeared on a large scale in people's homes. It was during the eighties that the Internet as we now know it was first developed. And it was during the 1980s that businesses, communication networks, air travel, and a host of other economic entities were deregulated, giving them a freer hand to cross borders and expand with fewer restrictions.

The Reagan Years

Nineteen eighty was a watershed year in American politics. When the decade began, the entire world was reeling from the shock of climbing energy prices, inflation, and record-high interest rates. People were working harder and their money was buying less. Unemployment was higher than at any time since World War II. Americans looked to their government for help and what they saw distressed them. President Jimmy Carter told them that no easy solutions could be found, that they should lower their expectations and learn to live with less.

When Republican Ronald Reagan stepped onto the national political stage in 1980, he revived the hopes of many Americans. Reagan insisted there *were* simple solutions—just cut taxes, deregulate business, and pump billions into American military might. The rest would take care of itself. Reagan was handily elected president, and he swept a Republican (GOP) majority into the Senate for the first time in twenty-five years.

The Reagan years became known as the "go-go" eighties. The government abolished thousands of regulations on business and cut billions of dollars in taxes. Huge sums of money

The administration of President Ronald Reagan dominated the 1980s. Reagan's pro-business stance ushered in an era called the "go-go" eighties.

were diverted from social programs and into a massive military buildup that included research into high-tech weapons such as the Strategic Defense Initiative (SDI), or "Star Wars," and the B-2 Stealth bomber.

Reagan's can-do attitude improved consumer confidence. The stock market soared. Car sales went up. Home sales increased. Hundreds of businesses grew and changed in waves of takeovers and mergers. Deregulated savings and loan institutions (S&Ls) went on a building spree, erecting hundreds of gleaming office buildings, strip malls, and hotels.

Apple founder John Scully is flanked by co-founders Steve Jobs and Steve Wozniak Jr. They are shown in 1984 with the Apple IIc, a remarkably small computer at the time. Apple was committed to making the personal computer affordable to the average consumer.

On the West Coast, an entire new industry was built in Redmond, Washington, and Silicon Valley in Sunnyvale, California. Bill Gates of Microsoft and the two Steves—Wozniak and Jobs—of Apple were fulfilling the dream of putting personal computers in every home. Startup companies responded to the sudden demand for hardware such as wires, printers, and modems along with software, floppy disks, and other computer support. People were changing the basic way business was conducted and getting rich doing it.

The End of the Cold War

While the American economy was booming half a world away, the Soviet Union was floundering. Seventy years of bloated command-economy communism—the government controlled all resources and manufacturing—had not provided the Soviet people with basic human necessities such as adequate food, clothing, and shelter. The government was in a shambles, in part because three Soviet leaders had died within three years. When Mikhail Gorbachev came to power in 1985, relations between the USSR and United States were strained and distant, a dangerous situation for the two superpowers, each of which had thousands of nuclear missiles pointed at the other ready to launch at a moment's notice.

The eighties were tense times in the cold war. Reagan had called the Soviet Union an "evil empire" and deployed hundreds of medium-range nuclear missiles in Europe capable of reaching Moscow within minutes. The Soviets shot down a South Korean passenger jet that strayed over their airspace, killing all aboard, including dozens of Americans. A Soviet nuclear power plant had exploded at Chernobyl, spewing radioactivity across Europe. And the superpowers were supporting various proxy wars in Central America, Angola, Afghanistan, and elsewhere.

As the 1980s drew to a close, however, the cold war came to a sudden and unexpected halt. In Germany, on November 9–11, 1989, the Berlin Wall, which had separated the Communist-controlled east side of Berlin from the democratic, capitalist west side for more than a quarter century, was torn down. For the first time in more than forty-two years, Soviet troops were pulling out of Poland, Hungary, Romania, Czechoslovakia, and Bulgaria. These countries, which had been under strict Communist control since the end of World War II, became free to run their own governments and economies. The republics that made up the Soviet Union declared independence. The cold war, the war that never quite happened, was over.

While Germans, Bulgarians, and Hungarians danced in the streets over their new freedoms, Americans were not quite sure what to do. After fifty years of preparing to fight World War III with the Soviet Union, the United States was suddenly the only superpower in the world. The Central Intelligence Agency and the Pentagon were unprepared for victory. Hundreds of private companies that employed hundreds of thousands of people to build military hardware were looking at layoffs and even bankruptcy.

The Bush-Quayle Years

George Bush was elected president in 1988 with J. Danforth Quayle as vice president. The 1988 election followed recent trends that showed fewer eligible voters casting their votes. In the

1988 election only 50 percent of Americans over age eighteen actually voted.

Bush had been Reagan's vice president for eight years, and his policies were a continuation of Reaganomics and deregulation. Bush's pledge during the 1988 campaign was endlessly repeated: "Read my lips; no new taxes!" Unfortunately, some of the economic practices of the Reagan years were starting to cause problems.

The tax cuts, the military buildup, and unchecked domestic spending had tripled the national debt. That meant the government was spending hundreds of billions more than it was taking in in taxes. The national debt in the eighties had climbed from $914 billion in 1980 to $2.8 trillion in 1988.

Study after study showed that Reaganomics had benefited the wealthy more than the poor and middle class. As the decade closed, the American economy was undergoing a transition from a manufacturing base to a service base: Thousands of people lost their jobs in waves of plant closings and so-called corporate downsizing. By summer 1989, economic problems could no longer be ignored.

The deregulation of the S&Ls had fueled a countrywide failure of those institutions. On August 9, 1989, Congress was forced to enact a $166 billion bailout bill to prevent the U.S. banking system from collapsing. In 1990, George Bush was forced to renege on his "no new taxes" pledge and sign into law the biggest tax increase in U.S. history. Meanwhile, the country began slipping into a two-year recession.

Problems Abroad

While Americans worried about the economy, political crises erupted abroad. In May 1989, Americans watched as students in Communist China—inspired by events in Russia—held prodemocracy rallies in Beijing's Tiananmen Square. George Bush, a former ambassador to China, promoted friendly relations with the country. But Chinese troops attacked the demonstrators with tanks, violently crushing the prodemocracy movement. In a move criticized by many, Bush continued to make friendly overtures to China despite the massacre of the demonstrators.

Closer to home, another muddy moral situation occurred in Panama. During the cold war years, the United States had been a strong supporter of Panamanian dictator Manuel Noriega. The Panamanian strongman had been on the CIA payroll for decades, including the years George Bush was the agency's director. But by the 1980s Noriega was protecting international

A group of journalists marches in Tiananmen Square in China in support of student protests asking for civil rights in 1989. The protests were brutally suppressed.

drug traffickers and allowing their profits to be laundered through Panamanian banks.

On December 20, 1989, U.S. troops invaded Panama and tried to capture Noriega. More than three thousand innocent civilians were killed in the attack. Noriega hid in the Vatican embassy for days but was finally captured and jailed in Florida. Fighting a small, deadly war to capture one man raised questions about the priorities and goals of the American military.

As the eighties drew to a close, the stage was set for a new world order. With the Soviet Union all but dissolved, China was emerging as an economic superpower that could ignore the United States at will. The U.S. military was scaling down for smaller missions with narrowly defined goals, such as invading Panama to slow drug trafficking. American workers were moving away from an economy based on building fighter jets and submarines and moving toward one based on microchips and floppy disks. And after ten years of Republicans in the White House, millions were ready for a Democratic administration.

Chapter One

President Bill Clinton delivers his inauguration speech at the Capitol on January 20, 1997. Clinton was voted into office in 1992 after the American people became frustrated with George Bush's inability to solve the country's economic problems.

Big Changes in Washington

In 1990, Iraqi dictator Saddam Hussein invaded the oil-rich country of Kuwait in the Persian Gulf. He threatened to take over Saudi Arabia, which would have given Iraq control of 20 percent of the world's oil reserves. President Bush put together an international coalition to stop Saddam called Operation Desert Storm. By the end of February 1991, the U.S. military and Allied armies had driven Iraq out of Kuwait.

The success of Desert Storm left Americans exhilarated: Saddam Hussein was no longer seen as a threat, and the conflict had resulted in few American casualties. As American soldiers marched in victory parades across America, George Bush's approval ratings soared to a remarkable 90 percent.

Bush's reelection in 1992 looked like a sure thing.

But something happened on the way to the election. Although the 1989 recession had officially ended in 1991, Americans had grown accustomed to a daily news diet of layoffs, bankruptcies, dismal economic forecasts, and long lines of job applicants. The unemployment rate jumped from 5.3 percent in 1989 to 7.5 percent just before the 1992 election.

Together, the big three automakers—Chrysler, Ford, and General Motors (GM)—lost $5 billion in 1991. General Motors had laid off 74,000 workers in 1992 alone. Other large corporations were also instituting massive layoffs. AT&T laid off 40,000 workers; IBM fired 60,000. Scott Papers fired 11,000 people. When people lost their jobs they also lost their benefits. Between 1991 and 1992, over 2 million people lost health insurance, increasing the number of uninsured people to 37.4 million.

There were other economic problems as well. During the layoffs, many companies replaced older managers with younger ones. This caused a wave of age discrimination cases in the courts, an increase of 32 percent between 1989 and 1992. Other jobs were permanently lost to automation, more efficient plant operation, and the export of jobs to foreign countries to take advantage of cheaper labor costs. The recession was over and the economy was improving, but newspapers called it a "jobless recovery." With this sort of media pessimism, even people who held onto their jobs felt insecure.

Although President George Bush's popularity grew with the success of Desert Storm, his lack of solutions to America's economic problems led to his defeat to Clinton in 1992.

As the country geared up for the 1992 presidential election, people were looking for a candidate with an appealing vision for America. Polls showed that people considered the budget deficit—now approaching $4 trillion—to be one of the nation's top problems. Another problem was the rising cost of consumer goods.

In 1980, an average home sold for $64,000. By 1993, that same home was selling for $121,000.

The number of Americans living below the poverty line reached 14.5 percent—the highest level in thirty years as the gap between rich and poor continued to widen. It has been said that Americans vote their pocketbooks. George Bush was an easy target for people's economic frustrations.

The 1992 Presidential Race

Bush was a foreign affairs expert. He had faced down the Iraqis and grappled with the collapse of communism in Eastern Europe. But on the domestic side, he was dealt a huge budget deficit and an unfriendly Democratic-controlled Congress that would not pass his programs. On television, people felt that Bush failed to articulate what he himself called "the vision thing."

Bush's advisers scrambled to give the president a well-defined action plan. A presidential trip to the Far East was changed from a foreign policy mission to one that would show the president's concern for American jobs. Bush took along U.S. industrialists to pressure Japan to buy more American products. Instead of projecting an image of strength, however, Bush succumbed to jet lag and prescription medications. At a state dinner he became ill, vomited into the lap of the Japanese prime minister, and briefly passed out. This unfortunate image colored public perceptions of his trip and of his candidacy. Meanwhile, back home a generation of "new" Democrats was sharpening its political strategy for the next campaign.

William Jefferson Clinton first appeared on the national political stage when he gave a long speech at the 1988 Democratic National Convention. Bill Clinton was the governor of Arkansas, and he had a message. Democrats, he said, "have to articulate a

Bill Clinton achieved a presidential victory largely on his message that he would fix the economy. The Bush campaign's attacks on Clinton's character largely backfired.

philosophy that is not perceived as too liberal. The American people are deeply conservative in general and very progressive in particular."[1]

Although Bush's approval rating had skidded, the traditional incumbent advantage still made him the front-runner for reelection in 1992. The Re-

Ross Perot

During the spring and summer of 1992 the presidential campaign became a three-way race. Texas billionaire Ross Perot, who had made a fortune in computer programming, ran as an independent candidate. Perot seemed to have answers to the American people's questions. As a political outsider, he promised to return the country to its rightful "owners," the people. He argued that the federal deficit had to be slashed, the nation's manufacturing base had to be rebuilt, and U.S. factories should stop moving to Mexico where labor was cheap.

Perot developed a strong following. By April 1992 his approval rating had climbed to 30 percent in the opinion polls. By July he was running ahead of Clinton. He was, however, extremely unpredictable. On July 16, Perot abruptly withdrew from the race after claiming that men working for President Bush were planning to disrupt his daughter's impending wedding. Then, after his supporters urged him to reconsider, he rejoined the race on October 1. Using his billions to finance his campaign, Perot bought thirty-minute blocks of television time to discuss budget deficits and job creation.

But Perot's erratic behavior turned off many of his supporters. When the votes were counted in November, the Texas businessman had received only 19 percent of the total. Nevertheless, this was the best showing of a third-party candidate in seventy years.

When Perot ran again in the 1996 election, however, Americans were even less enamored; he received only 9 percent of the votes cast.

Ross Perot injected a new vitality into the idea of a third-party candidacy—until he withdrew from the running and then decided to run again—causing him to lose credibility with the American people.

publicans had, after all, won five of the past six presidential races.

Clinton emerged during the Democratic primaries as the strongest candidate to run against Bush. After his nomination, Clinton chose Tennessee senator Albert Gore as his running mate. The dominant theme of Clinton's campaign was to be the economy. So that no one on his staff would forget what the campaign was about, Clinton strategists posted a sign in his headquarters that read "It's the economy, stupid!" The campaign was literally waged over bread-and-butter issues. In one televised debate, Clinton scored public approval for knowing the price of a loaf of bread. Bush lost points when he expressed amazement at an electronic price scanner in a supermarket—he hadn't shopped for his own groceries in years.

The Bush campaign countered with hardball political tactics. It was revealed that as a college student Clinton had tried marijuana, avoided the military draft, and protested the war in Vietnam. Charges were also made public that he had had extramarital affairs. The Republicans made the issue of character a central part of their campaign strategy.

Clinton Is Elected

But while Bush was talking about character issues, Americans wanted to hear about economy, crime, and health care. During several preelection televised debates, Clinton appeared charismatic, relaxed, friendly, and in charge, and his focus on economic issues paid off. In November he sailed to a landslide 370 electoral votes to Bush's 168. The popular vote was narrower—43 percent for Clinton, 37.5 for Bush.

Bill Clinton was the first "baby-boom" president. He was also the first president elected since World War II who had not fought in that conflict. Baby-boom rock bands such as Fleetwood Mac, whose song "Don't Stop Thinking About Tomorrow" had become Clinton's campaign theme song, performed at his inaugural ball. But one trend did not make the Democrats smile. During the election, they had lost ten congressional seats to Republicans even as the Democrats won the White House. This trend would hurt the party seriously in 1994.

Unfortunately for the new president, he enjoyed no traditional honeymoon period during which the media and Congress spared him criticism. During the campaign, Clinton had appealed to gay voters by promising to allow homosexuals into the military. When he tried to implement that policy as president, the White House was deluged with phone calls and letters expressing vociferous opposition.

MTV Rocks the Vote

The 1992 presidential election had an extra twist—it was covered by MTV. Since 1990 the music video channel had been running the Rock the Vote commercial campaign with big-name rock stars encouraging young people to vote. During the campaign, MTV assigned reporter Tabitha Soren, twenty-four, to cover the election. It was a risky move because no one knew if MTV viewers would be interested in presidential politics, or if the candidates would take a rock video network seriously. But in a move that shocked even the network, all of the candidates granted access to Soren. They saw the value in reaching America's younger voters. Audience reaction was positive. For the next several months, under the "Choose or Lose" banner, Soren interviewed all of the contenders.

The battle between Bush and Clinton represented two generations squaring off against each other. Bush was sixty-seven and Clinton was forty-five. When MTV proposed a televised "town meeting" at which candidates could answer the questions of young voters, Bush said he would not appear on the "teenybopper network." Only Clinton expressed interest. After ninety minutes of issues-oriented questions—with a few rock music queries thrown in—Clinton was a hit with MTV viewers. He even promised to come back once he was elected.

Voter turnout in 1992 among young voters jumped more than 20 percent from the 1988 election. While MTV couldn't take total credit, a joke going around the music industry said "MTV broke three acts in 1992. Pearl Jam, Arrested Development . . . and Bill Clinton."

Right-wing talk show hosts and Republicans in Congress united against Clinton on this issue. This opposition was a warm-up for what would become a protracted battle over another Clinton issue, health care.

Health Care Reform

During the campaign, health care reform topped Clinton's agenda. Although previous presidents from Theodore Roosevelt to Harry Truman had addressed problems in the health care system, serious reform had not occurred. But the issue had become so prevalent by 1992 that reform was supported by the American Medical Association (AMA), the powerful physicians' lobby that had long opposed universal health insurance.

The number of Americans without health insurance had grown to 37 million. Unchecked federal health care costs—already 25 percent of the federal budget—were expected to triple by 2030. Polls showed ordinary Americans were dissatisfied with the existing system. Health care costs in 1994 comprised 14 percent of the total American economy. That number was expected to climb to 20 percent by 2000. Public interest groups and politicians alike said it was time for a change. But everyone, it seemed, had a different plan for reform.

Clinton had stressed to voters during the campaign that if he were elected, Americans would also get Hillary Rodham Clinton's expertise as a valuable benefit. During the health care reform debate, Clinton appointed his wife to head a task force to draft an overhaul of the system. Mrs. Clinton would be the unpaid chairwoman of the Task Force on National Health Care Reform. Some experts in the field welcomed the First Lady's appointment, but others cautioned against it, including Bruce Smith, professor of public administration at Columbia University, as quoted by an Associated Press writer:

"It is always a mistake to give such prominence to a team trying to devise policy in so difficult an area. You have to grind through the options and make tough choices, and it's hard to do at a high political level," he said, especially since any

Hillary Clinton speaks on health care reform before Congress. President Clinton's emphasis on national health care did not gain widespread public support and ultimately stalled in Congress.

health reform plan is likely to hurt many people—cutting benefits and increasing costs for some, raising deductibles, limiting Medicare payments, reducing doctors' incomes.[2]

Clinton's proposals included capping health care costs, promoting managed care competition, and forcing doctors and hospitals to keep costs down through utilization review. He also advocated creating new health alliances that would mean restricted choices of doctors and services for some while broadening the availability of health care for the uninsured.

This was the most ambitious domestic policy experiment since Social Security was enacted in the 1930s. Politicians were as concerned about the details as were leaders of business and the health care professions. Average citizens began to worry that they might be harmed rather than helped by a cumbersome new federal program.

Some very powerful organizations aligned to cast doubt on the Clintons' health care reform package. Among them was the Health Insurance Association of America, which sponsored a $10 million television ad campaign featuring a fictional middle-class couple, Harry and Louise. The commercial showed the two sitting in their kitchen, worrying aloud about whether they would be able to retain their family physician if a huge government bureaucracy instituted a health care reform plan. The commercial generated over 260,000 calls to its 800-number and helped sink Clinton's plan when the administration failed to rebut the argument that health care reform would hurt people who were already insured.

In the summer of 1994, polls showed a majority of Americans supporting the idea of universal health care. But less than half supported Clinton's plan. And the president's popularity was slumping in the polls. By October Clinton had given up on his health care agenda. At that time he was occupied with another problem—the midterm congressional elections of 1994.

The Republican Takeover of Congress

Voters were unkind to George Bush in 1992, and they were not feeling any better in 1994 when they went to the polls to vote for congressional candidates and governors. But they seemed to take out their frustrations on a man who was not even on the ballot—Bill Clinton. In state after state, voters cast out Democrats—some of whom had served in Congress for decades—and rewarded Republicans. Republicans picked up seats across the board in

Bill Clinton's decreasing popularity in 1994 led to a voter backlash in Congress when the public voted into office a Republican majority in one of the lowest election turnouts in American history.

Senate, House, gubernatorial, state legislature, and even mayoral races.

Polls showed that more than half the voters said they were no better off than they had been in 1992. A quarter said things were worse. Clinton's approval rating was about 44 percent, with 51 percent disapproving of his White House performance. In southern states, the numbers were far worse for the president. Voters expressed wide disapproval with congressional performance and overwhelming support for term limits. So they turned on Democrats who had been running the country for most of their lifetimes.

> "Not since 1952 have Republicans controlled the United States Congress," said Sen. Bob Dole of Kansas. "That's when Eisenhower was elected president, the Dodgers were still in Brooklyn, and a postage stamp cost 3 cents.
>
> "One hundred and fifty-five million Americans have been born since Republicans last controlled the United States Congress," the Senate GOP leader said. They had the Senate for six years until 1986; last held the House in 1954.[3]

The new Senate of January 1995 was composed of 52 Republicans and 48 Democrats. House membership comprised 230 Republicans and 204 Democrats. The Democrats also lost ten governorships, giving the Republicans 30 states and the Democrats 19, with one independent. In addition, the Democrats lost control of the legislatures in six states.

These results came out of one of the worst-attended elections in history. Sixty-four percent of eligible voters (Americans eighteen and older) did not vote at all. Of the 193 million Americans of voting age, only 36 percent felt it was worthwhile to cast their vote. The Republicans garnered a little over half of the total votes cast, meaning their rise to power was carried by under 20 percent—or one in five—eligible voters in the country.

The Contract with America

Many credit the success of the Republicans in 1994 to the man who became Speaker of the House, Newt Gingrich. Gingrich, it was said, had been planning for this moment since childhood; even in high school he talked about the day when he would break the Democrats' lock on Congress.

When Gingrich arrived in Washington as a congressman from Georgia in 1979, the Republicans had been out of power for twenty-three years. But he refused to "get used to" the minority status of his party. Dubbed "Newtron" for his penchant for verbal bomb throwing, in 1988 he brought down popular Democratic Speaker of the House Jim Wright on ethics charges.

Gingrich spent a full ten years methodically recruiting and training a corps of loyal followers. In 1986 he took over as chairman of GOPAC, a political action committee dedicated to getting more Republicans into state and local offices. He held weekly conferences with GOP candidates, mailed them instructional audiotapes with such titles as "Go Negative Early," "Don't Try to Educate," and "Never Back Off," and appeared in person during their campaign rallies.

GOPAC's coaching helped get GOP candidates elected and honed the Republicans' message so as to hit the same themes in similar terms across the country and in general convey an impression of party unity. According to *Time* magazine:

> Divisive issues such as abortion were explicitly avoided; the focus was on strategy, not philosophy. Gingrich taught his acolytes "our rhythm and style," how to use his serrated language to cut their opponents; Democrats were to be described as traitors and with such adjectives as sick, corrupt, bizarre. Gingrich eventually became such a cult figure among young Republicans that supporters considered publishing a comic book with him as a hero fighting bureaucratic bloat.[4]

Gingrich's work with GOPAC led him to develop a ten-point plan that would broadcast his message to the American people loud and clear. He called it the Contract with America. On September 27, 1994, closing in on the elections, 350 Republican candidates gathered on the steps of the Capitol building. Amid red, white, and blue banners, each candidate signed the Contract with America.

House Republican leader Newt Gingrich and his Republican colleagues gather to sign Gingrich's Contract with America—a ten-item program that Gingrich promised the American people he and his colleagues would guarantee.

Each of the ten items on the list had registered at least a 60 percent public approval rating in focus group tests. They included vows to pass a balanced budget amendment; limit constitutional appeals for criminals; enact tough welfare reform; grant tax credits for adoption; grant an extra $500-per-child tax credit to wage earners; provide more funds for the military; cut capital gains taxes; and enact term limits for Congress.

After the GOP swept into power, Gingrich promised to enact all of the contract's ten points within one hundred days. Ninety-three days later, only term limits had failed—a favorite of the public, but a death sentence to politicians like Gingrich who had been in power for years. In the process, Gingrich became one of the most talked about people in America. His influence was reflected in *Time* magazine's choice of Gingrich as Man of the Year in 1995.

Clinton Is Reelected

The twists and turns of American politics in the 1990s could not be easily predicted. When the Republicans took over Congress in 1994, it looked like Bill Clinton would be a one-term president. But many opposed the GOP's views on women's issues, social programs, and the environment. Voters began to look kindly on Clinton as a moderating force in the Republican revolution.

Then in the winter of 1995 congressional Republicans tried to push Clinton to approve the budget bill. When the president would not give in, Congress refused to appropriate funds to keep the government running. The shutdown of the federal government made headlines and opinion polls showed widespread disapproval of Republican tactics. The situation was made worse by Gingrich's admission that he forced the impasse partly due to a perceived presidential snub during former Israeli prime minister Yitzhak Rabin's funeral. Gingrich's star began to fade.

When Republican Bob Dole picked up the mantle to run for president, Clinton's popularity was already on the upswing. Once again, the Republicans tried to make character an issue in the campaign. Once again the strategy failed.

In 1996, Clinton became the first Democrat to be reelected to the presidency since 1944. But in a strong commitment to the status quo, it was also the first Republican Congress to be reelected since 1930. In 220 years of American government, no Democratic president had been reelected to the White House while the opposition party was controlling Congress.

In a blistering campaign in which the two parties spent half a billion dollars, voters sent a strong message: People didn't trust either party enough to let them run the country without

Republican presidential candidate Bob Dole lost the presidential election bid to Clinton in 1996.

opposition. Voters elected a moderate Democrat as president to carry out a moderate Republican agenda. But once again, many showed apathy toward all politics. Less than 50 percent bothered to vote—the lowest turnout in a presidential election since 1924.

In the end, Clinton received 379 electoral votes as opposed to Dole's 159. In the popular vote, Clinton received 50 percent of all votes cast; Dole, 41 percent; and Ross Perot, 9 percent.

Welfare Reform

One of the major Republican charges against Clinton was that the president took traditional Republican issues and made them his own. This was shown most clearly on the issue of welfare re-

Clinton takes the oath of office for a second time in 1997. Clinton's moderately conservative agenda won him popularity among the majority of voters.

form. In prior years no Democrat would have promised to "change welfare as we know it." But Clinton was a so-called New Democrat who believed Democrats had to moderate their more liberal tendencies to gain and keep the support of the majority of the public. At the same time, Republicans learned that if they wanted to stay in power, they needed to move some of their more extreme conservative positions to the center.

The Republican move to the center became obvious in 1996 when a bipartisan vote raised the minimum wage from $4.25 to $5.15 an hour. Republicans also helped pass the Kennedy-Kassebaum health bill, which made all health insurance portable from job to job and curtailed exclusions based on preexisting medical conditions.

Nothing demonstrated the Democratic tilt to the right more than the Personal Responsibility and Work Opportunity Act of 1996, commonly known as welfare reform. This bill profoundly affected the lives of more than 13 million Americans, many of them children.

Under the new system, the head of most families on welfare would have to find work within two years or face the loss of benefits. After two years, able-bodied adults unable to find private sector work might be offered community-service jobs if states and localities wanted to pay for them. While Clinton insisted on some child-care support and the continuation of federally funded health care for the poor (Medicaid), the bill provided no funds for public jobs. Each state would get a lump sum of money called a block grant, which it would allocate to a welfare program deemed best suited to its needs, and a total savings of $56 billion would come from denying eligibility to legal immigrants and from reducing food-stamp allocations.

The most striking provisions were that no American could receive more than five years' worth of welfare in a lifetime, that single mothers on welfare who refuse to cooperate in identifying the fathers of their children could lose at least 25 percent of their benefits, and that unmarried teen mothers were eligible for benefits only if they stayed at home and in school. States were permitted some leeway in making these requirements tougher or more lenient. States that failed to move 20 percent of their caseloads from welfare to work by the end of 1997—and 50 percent by 2002—would face cutbacks in their block grants, and thus less money to distribute to the poor.

The welfare reform bill was signed during a booming economy when unemployment was at an historic low. No one—neither the politicians nor the social scientists toiling away on their studies—knew what would happen if the economy went into a tailspin, jobs became scarce, and working people were forced to go onto the welfare rolls.

Changes in Washington?

The adage "The more things change, the more they stay the same" might have been applied to American politics in the 1990s. Although the Republicans gained a majority in Congress for the first time in a generation, and a Democratic president was reelected, the sources of power and money that ruled Washington in 1999 were the same as in 1989 and even 1979. Big business poured billions into the campaign coffers of politicians, and the needs and wants of the common citizens were given lip service, but largely ignored.

Most Americans wanted their government to take care of the people's business. But by the late 1990s, Congress was bogged down in typical partisan bickering. The Republicans made dozens of charges against Clinton concerning campaign contributions, land deals in Arkansas, and his private sex life.

A special prosecutor, Kenneth Starr, was appointed to investigate Clinton, and for more than four years and $50 million, Starr pried into every aspect of the president's personal and political life. But it seemed the more Starr tried to reveal about Clinton, the less Americans seemed to care. In the end, Bill Clinton's sex life grabbed more headlines than welfare reform, the Clean Air Act, and the balanced budget. In light of this, few people were surprised when voting levels sank to all-time lows, and people simply decided that politics in Washington had little to do with their lives.

Chapter Two

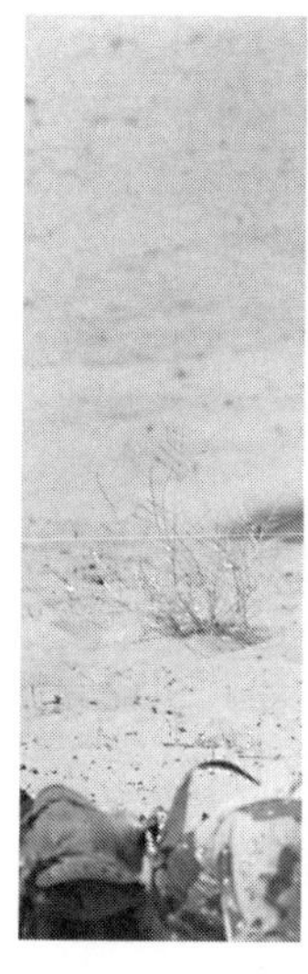

American troops train in the Saudi desert during Operation Desert Storm. The war was the first to be fully televised and featured new technology.

The Post–Cold War World

With the fall of the Berlin Wall in November 1989 and the collapse of the Soviet Union two years later, the United States was left as the world's reigning superpower. This political shuffle ushered in an era that George Bush called a "new world order where diverse nations are drawn together in a common cause."[5]

But the new world produced several deadly regional conflicts and in some cases, anarchy. Ironically, the simple polarity of communism versus capitalism had lent stability to world politics. Once that polarity ended, political disorder became more complicated than in the past.

As the nineties progressed, U.S. foreign policy became driven by the desire to support economic and political reforms in formerly Communist countries. The new goal was to advance American economic interests. Russia and China were huge, untapped markets for American goods, but also possibly dangerous economic rivals. To insure smooth relations with these large countries, the United States used trade agreements and economic pressure instead of military threats.

Meanwhile, regional—but potentially dangerous—conflicts erupted in such countries as Somalia, Haiti, and Bosnia. As these countries degenerated into anarchy, some response from the United States was expected. But most Americans, still remembering the lessons of Vietnam, had little desire to fight a war on foreign soil. So while many agonized over the scenes of devastation in these countries, no general consensus about what should be done emerged.

The Fall of the Soviet Union

The collapse of the Soviet Union was so total and complete that it dramatically changed the dynamics of American foreign policy. Most ordinary Russians were ill prepared to deal with the major economic and social changes that followed the Soviet Union's collapse. It was in the best interest of the United States to make sure that its former enemy survived to realize the goals of democracy and capitalism.

The Soviet Union had a long and bloody history. Its fifteen republics had made it the largest country in the world. From czarist rule to postrevolution Communist Party rule, power had always come from the top down, and was always exercised with an iron fist. After the collapse, many European countries feared a return of repressive Russian control in one form or another.

Fears were further complicated in August 1991. Mikhail Gorbachev, the Soviet premier, was about to sign a historic document freeing the fifteen Soviet republics and transferring authority for taxation, state security, and natural resources to local governments. On August 18, a special detachment of old-line Communist soldiers put Gorbachev under house arrest. The eight former military officers who were the coup leaders lamely announced to the world that Gorbachev was too old and sick to run the country.

Within hours, resistance to the coup was organized with Boris Yeltsin as its leader. Yeltsin climbed onto a tank in front of the Russian White House and called for a general strike. By August 20, the streets of Moscow were filled with 150,000 protesters. As the coup leaders organized airplanes and paratroopers for an armed assault on the protesters, people locked arms to form a human chain around the

Boris Yeltsin (center) was elected general secretary of the Soviet Union in 1991 after a coup temporarily drove Gorbachev from power.

White House where Yeltsin was staying. By the next day the coup had failed, as Soviet troops took the side of the resistance.

With crowds cheering and soldiers waving revolutionary flags, Gorbachev resumed control. Proving how much the world had changed in a few years, Western rock and roll music—which had been illegal in the Soviet Union—blared from Soviet radios. After the coup, the radio played messages of support from Mick Jagger of the Rolling Stones, along with former Beatle Ringo Starr and the Eurythmics' Dave Stewart. Soviet rock bands set up on the stairs to the White House and held a spontaneous rock concert.

New Problems for Russia

For three days, one of the world's superpowers had careened out of control. Eight men stepped out of the shadows to take control of the country's four-million-soldier army and thirty thousand nuclear warheads. When the coup crashed, seventy-five years of Communist rule dissolved into the dust. And Boris Yeltsin would soon be elected general secretary for his role in the coup.

As the nineties progressed, the Russian people began getting their first taste of democracy. Many did not like it. They were used to being told by the government where to live, where to work, and even what to think. Now, for the first time in a thousand years, they were asked to make major decisions affecting their economic and political life. Their state-run jobs were turned over to the free market, and unemployment, food shortages, and skyrocketing inflation quickly followed.

Where Communist bosses had once run black market cartels in everything from vodka to shoes, organized crime stepped in. Ancient ethnic rivalries between cultures threatened civil war in some republics. And Soviet nuclear weapons were suddenly the object of thieves trading in black market uranium. Yeltsin was forced to fight off another coup in December 1993.

To stave off another revolution, Bush and forty-two other countries ordered billions of dollars of aid for the wounded country of 300 million people.

But in the end, the collapse of the Soviet Union greatly diminished the threat of nuclear war with the United States. On Bush's orders, for the first time in over forty years, the U.S. military was told to "stand down" from nuclear alert.

The Death of Yugoslavia

The collapse of the Soviet Union led to an upsurge in ethnic warfare in the newly freed republics, especially Yugoslavia. Yugoslavia first became a country in 1918 as the Kingdom of Serbs, Croats, and Slovenes, a nation uniting the South Slavs on the Balkan Peninsula. The country broke apart during World War II but reunited under Communist dictator Josip Tito as a federation of six republics—Serbia, Croatia, Slovenia, Montenegro, Macedonia, and Bosnia-Herzegovina. The republics were united by a common ethnic background and related languages, but they were divided by dialects, alphabets, and religions.

When Tito died in 1980, Yugoslavia began to unravel. In 1990, the Croats and Slovenes booted out the Communists and tried to get out from under Serbian domination. Serbia, which maintained Communist rule, wanted to preserve a strong state, or at least protect Serbs outside Serbia from domination by other groups. Mean-

while, Bosnia-Herzegovina became a simmering cauldron of ethnic tensions between Bosnian Muslims, Serbs, and Croats.

Provocation came from all sides. Croatia threatened the rights of all Serbs. The Slovenes set up their own government. The Serbs refused to allow a Croat to take his turn as head of the federal presidency.

In February 1991, the Croat prime minister warned that Yugoslavia was about to explode. His warnings went unheeded. By August, 23 million Yugoslavs would find themselves in a bloody, brutal war. Outsiders did not understand the conflict. But those within Yugoslavia knew the war was ignited by a conglomerate of fanatical nationalists, political careerists, and malcontents who were betting that the outside world would not interfere with their open military aggression.

Ethnic Cleansing

The troubles started in Bosnia-Herzegovina in August 1992. First Muslim-owned businesses were closed or attacked. Mosques were destroyed and houses firebombed. Then local Serb officials offered Muslims a chance to flee. By that time, most Muslims were terrified and ready to go. The Serbs called this process, "ethnic cleansing" as Muslims were driven out of Serb-controlled parts of Bosnia. Others called it genocide—the systematic and planned extermination of an entire group of people. Areas the Serbs did not hold were subject to shelling and terrorist raids aimed at convincing Muslims to leave. Although Serbs make up about one-third of Bosnia's population of 4.3 million, they took control of two-thirds of the territory. In the process, an estimated 3 million Bosnians became refugees. These events were broadcast into American homes on a daily basis. As human rights activist Zlatko Dizadarevic writes:

A Bosnian woman weeps while holding the skull of her son who was killed by Muslim forces. In the ethnic violence, 3 million Bosnians became refugees.

> Our television sets, and then our print media, were conveying an all-too-familiar picture of mass killing: of emaciated men in [concentration] camps, mounting testimonies of the slaughter of civilians, and an added dimension of the systematic rape of women—all carried out under a clearly articulated policy of "ethnic cleansing."[6]

By 1993 the evening news was filled with distressing pictures from the capital city of Sarajevo. After thirteen months of Serb shelling and a viciously cold winter, the 350,000 inhabitants of Sarajevo were destitute.

Visitors who had been to Sarajevo before the war could not reconcile their memories of a cosmopolitan, gracious city with the destruction they witnessed now. Sarajevo, a medieval storybook village where the world had come together less than a decade earlier for the 1984 Winter Olympics, had become a war zone. Heaps of uncollected garbage smoldered in streets lined with shattered buildings. Apartments had been turned into hospitals and parks into makeshift cemeteries. Machine-gun fire and mortar blasts rattled day in and day out. Snipers sat up in the hills picking off citizens going about the daily toil of finding food, fuel, and water. Old men, women, and children were targeted just as readily as soldiers. Dizadarevic describes one week:

> For sixty uninterrupted hours they've been showering steel on our dear city, on our gardens and tree-lined streets, our courtyards and facades. In this inferno there is no truce, no rest, no abatement of the red-hot artillery pieces. . . . Death had installed himself on an assembly line and mocks us all without distinction.[7]

By October, the United Nations had released evidence that Serb soldiers had raped thousands of Muslim women in Bosnia as part of an official campaign of terror. The UN Security Council set up a commission to gather evidence of war crimes for use in prosecution before an international tribunal. Further investigations revealed the mass murder of Muslim villagers by Croat soldiers.

In an effort to stop the war, the UN banned arms sales to the region, but

The bodies of nine Bosnian Muslims lay side by side ready for identification by families who have lost relatives in the ethnic conflict. The bodies were part of those discovered in a mass grave that was thought to have contained Muslim victims of Serb forces.

this unintentionally gave the well-supplied Serbs an advantage over the Muslims. Meanwhile, fighting broke out between Muslims and Croats around Mostar. By 1993, UN and European Union (EU) negotiators were joined by the United States and Russia as they vainly tried to mediate a peace agreement. In 1994 more than twenty thousand peacekeepers were deployed in twenty locations throughout Bosnia in an attempt to reduce the level of violence and deliver humanitarian aid.

In spite of UN intervention, the fighting continued and peace negotiations failed. A breakthrough came in 1995 when Assistant Secretary of State Richard Holbrooke devised a partition plan in which 49 percent of Bosnia would go to the Bosnian Serb Republic and 51 percent to the Muslim-Croat Federation. Meeting in Dayton, Ohio, the presidents of Bosnia, Croatia, and Serbia agreed to the terms in November 1995. A peace accord was signed in Paris on December 14. By this time, over a hundred thousand people had been killed or were missing in the conflict.

The peace settlement was monitored by an international force of sixty thousand troops from approximately twenty-five countries. The largest contingents were from the United States, Britain, France, and Russia.

Iraqi Invasion of Kuwait

While troubles stemming from independence movements and ethnic divisions in the Soviet Union grew, President Bush faced troubles at home. A looming financial crisis in 1990 forced him to raise taxes. Almost simultaneously, a crisis in a distant but strategically important land presented an entirely different challenge.

Iraqi president Saddam Hussein had fought a bloody war with Iran from 1980 to 1988. He was supported by tens of billions of dollars in aid from the United States and Middle Eastern

Iraqi president Saddam Hussein invaded Kuwait on August 2, 1990. The United States demanded that Hussein remove his occupying troops.

Arab oil states. But Saddam had grown resentful of his neighbors. He charged that while he protected them from Iran, they overproduced oil, undercutting the price Iraq could get for its oil. He charged the tiny oil-rich country of Kuwait in particular with stabbing Iraq in the back on this issue, but Saddam's reasoning masked Iraq's longtime territorial claims on Kuwait.

On July 24, 1990, thirty thousand Iraqi troops massed on the Kuwaiti border. Kuwait quickly agreed to Iraqi oil production quotas. But Saddam was not satisfied. On August 2, at 2 A.M., Iraq invaded Kuwait, which offered token resistance. Six days later, Iraq annexed Kuwait and issued this statement:

> The Revolutionary Command Council has decided to return the branch, Kuwait, to the whole and to the Iraq of its origins in a comprehensive and eternal merger.[8]

Bush labeled the invasion naked aggression and instituted a trade ban on Iraq. He also froze Iraq's and Kuwait's assets in the United States and

Kuwait Profile

Kuwait is a small desert kingdom made fabulously rich by the oil that lies under its sands. Baghdad had long claimed that the 6,880-square-mile country was part of Iraq. But since 1756 Kuwait has been ruled by the al-Sabah family as an emirate—a country ruled by a prince. More than half of Kuwait's population of 1.8 million are foreigners, mostly Arabian, including 300,000 Palestinians. Most Kuwaitis are Sunni Muslim, but about 30 percent belong to the rival Shiite sect.

Kuwait is considered by many to be a cultural center in the Middle East. Its newspapers are read throughout the Arab world, and it has long been a donor of economic aid to poorer countries inside and outside the Arab world. At the time of the Iraqi invasion, there were few democratic traditions to boast of, however. The country's parliament had been suspended in 1986 by emir Sheik Jaber al-Ahmed al-Sabah.

Kuwait's fleet of oil tankers was a frequent target of Iranian attacks during the Iran-Iraq war in the 1980s, in which Iran sporadically bombed Kuwait. Shiite Muslim terrorists, backed by Iran, carried out several successful terrorist attacks in Kuwait, including the bombing of the French and American embassies.

Kuwait lives on its vast oil reserves, which brought $30 billion to the country in 1983, but its economy has been in decline ever since. Before Iraq invaded, Kuwait produced about 1.5 million barrels of oil a day, and today owns about 12.5 percent of the world's reserves.

ordered aircraft carriers to the Persian Gulf. In a show of unity unheard-of during the cold war, the Soviet Union and the United States issued a joint statement condemning Iraq's actions. The Soviets had been Iraq's biggest arms suppliers, but they suspended sales of all military equipment. Saddam had Kuwait, but Iraq was isolated. Its only official supporter was the Palestine Liberation Organization (PLO), sworn enemy of Israel.

To gain support, Saddam called on fundamentalist Muslims to launch a jihad, or holy war, against foreign troops. He tied offers to withdraw from Kuwait to demands that Israel withdraw from its occupied territory claimed by the Palestinians. This put Israel into the middle of an international conflict.

Operation Desert Shield

George Bush used his skill in foreign affairs to organize an international opposition to Saddam Hussein. On August 8, he began U.S. troop deployment in the Persian Gulf. Throughout the month, the United States built up

General H. Norman Schwarzkopf (left) addresses troops during Operation Desert Storm. Schwarzkopf was the commander of U.S. joint forces in the Persian Gulf.

its ground forces in Saudi Arabia to one hundred thousand soldiers.

On August 25, the UN Security Council authorized use of force by the U.S. Navy against Iraq to prevent violations of UN economic sanctions. Saddam, however, had what analysts believed was the fourth largest army in the world and the potential support of vast numbers of fundamentalist Muslims. He threatened the West with international terrorism and menaced Israel to the point that U.S. airlines canceled flights to that country.

For his part, Bush was well aware that Americans would not endure another Vietnam-style war that dragged on for years in support of a questionable goal. Kuwait, after all, was an emirate, ruled by a prince, where democracy did not exist, and where women and foreign workers had no rights—women, for example, are not even allowed to drive cars in Kuwait. But American support for the action increased dramatically when gasoline prices shot up 30 percent almost overnight. Many believed Saddam was poised to take over Saudi Arabia, which would give him control of over 20 percent of the world's oil production.

Operation Desert Storm

On August 8, 1990, Bush addressed the nation with a televised message clearly intended for Saddam:

> We seek the immediate, unconditional and complete withdrawal of all Iraqi forces from Kuwait. . . . I cannot predict how long it will take to convince Iraq to withdraw from Kuwait. Sanctions will take time to have their full intended effect. But let it be clear: we will not let this aggression stand.[9]

To back up his words Bush organized an international coalition against Iraq. On November 29 the Security Council approved the use of military force against Iraq if it did not withdraw from Kuwait by January 15, 1991. Coalition members included Argentina, Australia, Bahrain, Bangladesh, Belgium, Canada, Czechoslovakia, Denmark, Egypt, France, Greece, Hungary, Italy, Kuwait, Morocco, the Netherlands, New Zealand, Niger, Norway, Oman, Pakistan, Poland, Qatar, Saudi Arabia, Senegal, South Korea, Spain, Syria, the United Arab Emirates, the United Kingdom, and the United States. It was the largest military action taken by the United States since the Vietnam War.

The United States took the unusual step of asking for international contributions of more than $53 billion to fight the war. Saudi Arabia and Kuwait were the largest donors. Two generals, H. Norman Schwarzkopf and Colin Powell, were assigned to lead an

American force of three hundred thousand U.S. troops who would fight alongside two hundred thousand other Allied troops.

The January 15 deadline passed and Saddam Hussein had not backed down. At 7 P.M. Eastern Standard Time on January 16, Bush declared: "The liberation of Kuwait has begun."[10]

Americans turned on their televisions to see the Iraqi capital of Baghdad light up under a hail of antiaircraft fire flashing across the night sky. For the next five weeks, intensive air attacks were carried out by eighteen hundred coalition fighter planes.

The coalition deployed technologically advanced weaponry, including the Tomahawk cruise missile, the Patriot antimissile system, advanced infrared targeting that illuminated Iraqi tanks buried in the sand, and aircraft never before tested in combat, such as British Tornadoes and U.S. F-117A Stealth fighters. The accuracy and firepower of these weapons simply overwhelmed Iraqi forces.

One of Iraq's first responses was the January 18 launching of surface-to-surface Scud missiles into Israel. To help Israel—which reluctantly remained neutral to appease U.S. concerns that the war would become an Arab-Israeli conflict—the United States deployed Patriot missiles in Israel to shoot down the Scuds. For the first time the Pentagon also deployed U.S. soldiers in Israel specifically to defend that country. Average citizens in Israel were frightened that Saddam would carry out threats to launch poison gas attacks. They were forced to live for days at a time in sealed rooms or cellars with gas masks close by. The Patriots intercepted or partially destroyed many of the approximately eighty-five missiles that Iraq fired against Saudi Arabia and Israel.

As the war progressed, the United States put its high-tech weapons on display. Every day, viewers could turn on television news shows and see Pentagon videotapes of the effects of "smart bombs" designed for pinpoint accuracy. The demonstrations garnered major support for the mission, but after the war it was revealed that only 7 percent of all bombs dropped were "smart." Some were remarkably accurate, but many missed their targets.

On February 13, Allied warplanes destroyed an underground structure in Baghdad, killing five hundred civilians. The United States expressed remorse at the civilian death toll but suggested that Saddam was to blame for his refusal to leave Kuwait.

As international debate over the war's costs and tactics escalated, the United States pounded the war zone,

Colin Powell

The Pentagon planned strict control of the media coverage of Operation Desert Storm. It was intense, dramatic, and brought into American living rooms live, via satellite. The Pentagon held daily briefings where generals and spokespersons would show videotapes of successful bombings along with graphs and charts plotting the war's progress. Colin Powell, one of the more charismatic generals, became an overnight celebrity because of his TV exposure.

General Colin Powell became a popular figure during Operation Desert Storm. He retired from his post on the Joint Chiefs of Staff in 1993 and did not take up the political life that many people wanted him to pursue.

Powell was the first African American to be named Chairman of the Joint Chiefs of Staff, the top military authority in the United States. He was the son of Jamaican immigrants who settled in the South Bronx. Powell fought in Vietnam, where he received a Bronze Star for saving two friends from a burning helicopter. He rose straight and fast through the military ranks and served as a national security adviser during the last year of Ronald Reagan's presidency. He was named head of the Joint Chiefs by President Bush in October 1989.

Powell's term ended in 1993. He was approached by both Republicans and Democrats to run for president, but declined to enter the political arena. His popularity remains high, however, and he is considered a serious contender for high public office, even the presidency.

sometimes surpassing twenty-eight hundred bombing missions in a single day. About one-third of the missions were meant to "soften up" targets in southern Iraq and Kuwait where Iraqi troops were dug into bunkers from which they were expected to lead the ground offensive against the Allied troops.

The Ground War

On February 24, Allied forces launched a broad, multipronged assault on Iraqi forces that lasted exactly one hundred hours. As part of the offensive, coalition troops engaged in a complicated series of diversionary tactics and feigned assaults to deceive Iraqi commanders. When the action began, the Pentagon instituted a temporary news blackout. Details of the battle were sketchy.

U.S. troops streamed into Kuwait while British forces invaded Iraq from Saudi Arabia. Thousands of French Foreign Legionnaires punched into southern Iraq and met little resistance. Schwarzkopf reported that Iraqi forces were light and over fifty-five hundred prisoners had been taken.

Five weeks of bombing had severely demoralized the Iraqi frontline troops, causing widespread desertions. Remaining frontline forces were quickly killed or taken prisoner with minimal coalition losses. Within hours, U.S. Marines surged into Kuwait and pushed within miles of Kuwait City. Col. John Stennick, chief of staff for the division, reported:

> Things are going very well. We thought we'd have to fight harder to get this far. The best news is that so few of our people have gotten hurt.[11]

On February 27, six weeks after it all began, the Persian Gulf War came to an end. White House spokesmen announced that the once-mighty Iraqi army was so devastated that to continue the war would lead to unnecessary killing. America's three hundred

After battle with U.S. soldiers, an Iraqi soldier lies dead in front of a disabled Soviet-made tank. Allied forces quickly subdued Iraq.

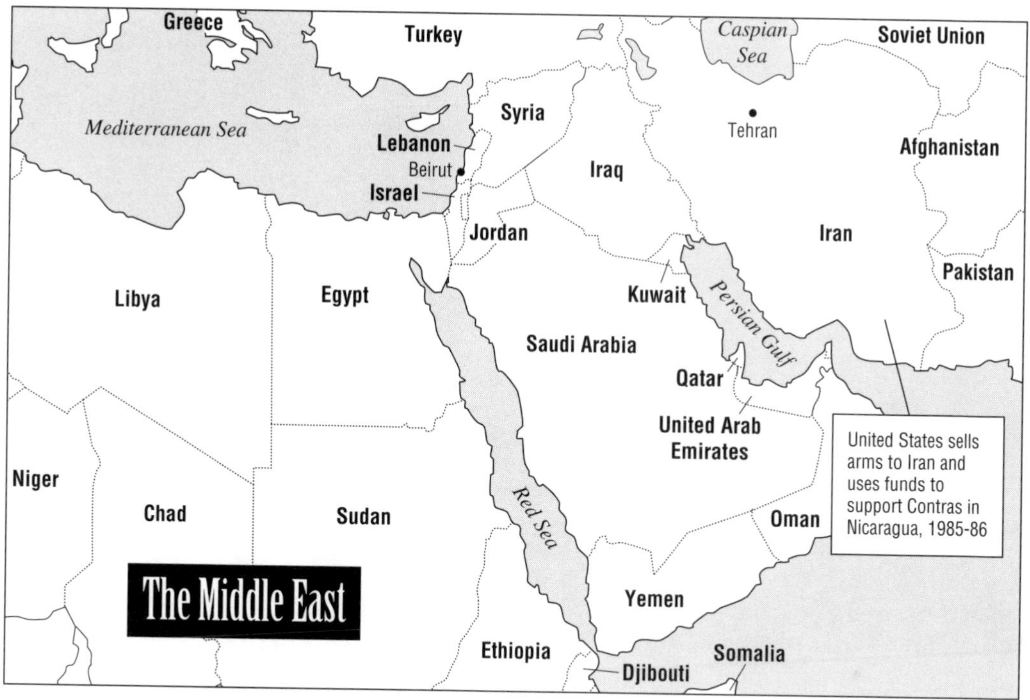

thousand troops could expect to come home within days.

The Final Toll

Joyful Kuwaitis reclaimed their country, but it was a country with a big problem. Iraq had blown up eight hundred of Kuwait's one thousand oil wells. American firefighters were dispatched to the region, where clouds of black, acrid smoke and raging oil fires filled the sky. The devastation had begun two days before the ground invasion when Iraqis touched off explosives placed at each well. Costs to cap and repair the wells were estimated at $20 billion over a five-to-ten-year period. Kuwait estimated that Iraq destroyed about 189 million gallons of oil a day—twice the daily consumption of Great Britain.

The skies over Kuwait were a dead, flat gray as the midday desert temperature dipped to forty degrees because heavy clouds of oil blocked the sun's rays. The flames from the burning oil wells shot two hundred feet into the sky and the intense heat could be felt from five hundred yards away.

In the end, the death toll for Allied forces was 340, of which 148 were Americans. Women also served in greater numbers and in more military roles than ever before; fifteen of the casualties were women.

Although Saddam was defeated by Allied forces, his presence in Kuwait continued to be felt because of the destruction he wreaked on the nation, including setting Kuwait's oil wells ablaze.

Thousands of Kuwaitis died, but accurate Iraqi casualty figures were hard to pin down. In June 1991 the U.S. Defense Intelligence Agency (DIA) estimated that 100,000 Iraqi soldiers died, 300,000 were wounded, 150,000 deserted, and 60,000 were taken prisoner. DIA uncertainty led to cautions that the estimate could be off by as much as 50 percent. Many human rights groups claimed markedly higher numbers.

Millions of other people were displaced in the conflict, including ethnic Kurds and Yemenis. The ultimate cost to the environment was also impossible to figure. Oil pipelines broke, wells were set ablaze, and millions of tons of bombs blackened the natural environment. Environmentalists considered the Gulf War to be one of history's greatest pollution disasters.

The political repercussions were also long lasting. Desert Storm solidified America's role as a global leader and military superpower. The war rejuvenated the United Nations, where an unprecedented partnership between Washington and Moscow enabled nations to stand united against a common aggressor. Saddam himself clung to power, and continued to cause misery for his own people. The U.S. decision not to pursue and definitely topple him would long be debated.

Most Americans were proud of the stunning success made of the international coalition of Desert Storm. Saddam Hussein posed a clear threat to the world's oil supply, and he was defeated quickly and completely with little loss of Allied lives. The goal of the mission was clearly defined and U.S. troops were in and out of the region within a matter of months.

But the United States would be involved in other conflicts in the 1990s that were not as easily resolved. The end of the cold war left the United States and other major powers without a reliable compass to guide them in foreign conflicts. U.S. interests were not always clear and the questions of when and where the United States and UN should intervene militarily were increasingly difficult.

These questions grew more urgent as modern technology delivered instant news from distant lands via American television. Scenes of genocide, starvation, and political oppression caused concern and calls for action in democracies around the world.

During the 1990s, Americans seemed less than willing to get involved in conflicts in other countries. In May 1998, new fears of nuclear war were heightened as India began underground testing of nuclear bombs. India said it needed a nuclear deterrent because of security threats from China and Pakistan. Pakistan responded with its own tests. (China agreed in October 1994 to stop sending complete missiles to its Pakistani allies. But since then it has continued to ship bomb parts.)

The United States, Britain, Japan, and some other industrialized nations imposed economic and military sanctions on both India and Pakistan and urged both countries to sign the Comprehensive Test Ban Treaty and the Nuclear Non-Proliferation Treaty.

India's and Pakistan's nuclear breakout was a reminder that countries with less to lose—including North Korea and Iran—were also joining the nuclear club. And although fear of nuclear confrontation between the Soviet Union and the United States had been reduced, nuclear weapons continued to pose a long-range threat to people and nations across the globe.

Amid concerns about violence in distant lands, Americans in the 1990s became targets of another deadly force, one that was wielded by U.S. citizens who had become violently distrustful of their own government.

Chapter Three

In the tenth day of a standoff between ATF forces and the Branch Davidians, a sign outside the compound reads "God help us we want the press." The conflict was one of several between the U.S. government and members of the radical fringe that occurred in the 1990s.

Violence in America

Every era is marked by violence and discord and the 1990s was no exception. Violence in the nineties was distinguished by several well-publicized incidents that seemed to fit a theme of domestic terrorism. The 1990s militia movement was first propelled into the headlines in 1992, when a former Green Beret named Randall Weaver, forty-four, illegally sold two sawed-off shotguns to an FBI informant.

In 1983, Weaver, his wife Vicki, and their four children had moved from Iowa to the rugged panhandle of northern Idaho, where they bought several acres of land on Ruby Ridge and built a house. Weaver, who sold firewood for a living, believed in white separatism and various apocalyptic prophecies. Federal agents say he also trafficked in firearms.

In 1992 Weaver was indicted for illegal weapons sales but failed to appear in court. He retreated to his mountain home where for the next eighteen months he thwarted officials' attempts to arrest him peacefully. Federal agents mounted a long-range surveillance and hoped to lure Weaver away from his heavily armed stronghold.

On August 21 the waiting ended when three marshals armed with M-16s entered the Weaver compound. Kevin Harris, twenty-five, who was living with the Weavers, chased the marshals accompanied by Weaver's fourteen-year-old son, Samuel. What happened next was later disputed in court, but guns were fired; when the shooting stopped Marshal William Degan and Samuel were dead.

For the next ten days, more than two hundred law enforcement officers, led by the FBI, surrounded the Weavers' cabin. The day after the shootings, an FBI sniper fired two rounds into the residence. One shot and wounded Weaver, another killed Vicki and seriously wounded Harris. Harris, Weaver, and Weaver's three daughters surrendered the next day.

Randy Weaver confers with lawyer Gerry Spence at the Senate committee investigations into the raid on his home at Ruby Ridge, Idaho.

Troubles in Waco

Only a month after Bill Clinton was sworn into office, another conflict occurred. This time between government agents and a religious paramilitary group, blew up in Waco, Texas at the Branch Davidian cult's isolated compound.

For months federal agents had been tracking frequent shipments of firepower that they say amounted to four tons of ammunition and enough parts to assemble hundreds of automatic and semiautomatic weapons. In addition, a package full of hand grenades destined for the compound accidentally split open in the United Parcel Service (UPS) facility, alerting Bureau of Alcohol, Tobacco, and Firearms (ATF) agents to the illegal shipments.

On February 28, 1993, ATF agents then attempted to

serve a search warrant on the compound for illegal firearm sales. More than one hundred agents charged the house and were met with a hail of gunfire, pinning them down for forty-five minutes. Four ATF agents and six cult members were killed. Sixteen agents were wounded.

As news crews from across the globe descended on Waco, information filtered out about the Branch Davidians. The leader of the cult was a high school dropout, rock musician, and polygamist preacher named Vernon Howell, who said God had renamed him David Koresh. His message was "If the Bible is true, then I'm Christ."[12] The charismatic leader drew more than one hundred people to join him in an armed fortress near Waco to await the end of the world. Koresh claimed to have more than a dozen wives inside the compound, with whom he had had seventeen children.

Leader of the Branch Davidian cult, David Koresh believed that he was Jesus Christ. He and one hundred cult members occupied a compound in Waco, Texas.

For fifty-one days, America watched as two hundred FBI, ATF, and other federal agents held a stakeout in the fields around the compound. Meanwhile, on March 12, 1993, Janet Reno was sworn in as the new attorney general of the United States. On April 19, Reno approved an assault on the compound that left eighty-six men, women, and children of the Branch Davidians dead. The compound was loaded with guns and ammunition which exploded and engulfed the buildings in flames when agents attacked with armored vehicles and tear gas.

Intense criticism of the government raid erupted even before the ashes of the burned compound were cold. Many charged that the ATF had been more concerned with the media spotlight than with correctly evaluating the Davidians' intentions and capabilities. ATF officials said the raid failed because a phone call from a radio station

The World Trade Center Bombing

Terrorism had harmed Americans in foreign countries, but the FBI and other law agencies had long prided themselves on keeping it from American shores. That feeling of immunity was shattered just two days before the events at Waco, on February 26, 1993. In the concrete canyons of lower Manhattan, an American symbol of wealth and power was shattered by a bomb.

An explosion and fire ripped through the World Trade Center, killing two, injuring three hundred, and forcing the evacuation of the twin towers of the 110-story skyscraper. The 1,350-foot-tall buildings, the second and third tallest buildings in the world, house 100,000 workers. Shortly after noon, the towers began rumbling when a Ford Econoline van filled with explosives blew up in an underground parking garage. The blast ripped into a commuter train station under the building. The ceiling collapsed onto scores of riders and caused multiple fires. Within minutes most of the offices in the building were engulfed in thick black smoke.

Police and workers evacuate the World Trade Center after a bomb blast left two people dead and two hundred injured.

Telephones went dead and electrical power went off, leaving the building's 104 elevators useless. Workers covered their faces with damp cloths or paper towels and stumbled down the long, dark, smoky stairwells. It was a two-hour ordeal for those on the top floors who emerged onto the street vomiting with soot-covered faces, aching legs, and lungs burning with smoke.

A radical Muslim cleric was arrested a few weeks later when he tried to claim his deposit on the rental van that caused the explosion. Mohammed A. Salameh, twenty-five, and six others were eventually found guilty of conspiring to wage a "war of terrorism against the United States" and sentenced to life in prison.

almost an hour before the shooting began tipped Koresh off. Questions remained as to why the ATF did not try to arrest Koresh on the many occasions when he left the compound to jog, shop, or eat in local restaurants. And, many asked, with children in the buildings, why was the whole operation not treated as a delicate hostage situation? These questions were never fully answered, and Koresh sympathizers took a dark view of their government's actions in Waco.

The Growing Militia Movement

The events at Ruby Ridge in 1992 and Waco in 1993 dismayed and horrified most Americans. But they particularly enraged and infuriated the militia fringe, which viewed these incidents not as accidents or even criminal negligence but as deliberate acts in a conspiracy to deprive Americans of their liberty. The militia members believed that this plot was carried out by a shadowy, globalist conspiracy bent on instituting a so-called sinister New World Order.

As early as the 1970s and 1980s right-wing extremists claiming immunity from American laws and regulations were becoming more prevalent. Many of them identified themselves as belonging to the Posse Comitatus. They refused contact with the government and claimed they needed no driver's licenses or license plates for their cars. Comitatus members claimed an absolute constitutional and biblical right to travel freely and unconditionally. They also claimed that there was no crime unless there was a victim—thus, for instance, speeding could not be a crime, nor could driving a car without a license plate. They believe that any judge that convicted them on these charges would be violating their constitutional rights and could be tried for treason.

Militia members hold several beliefs in common to varying degrees—from rational to strictly racist. Some think the federal government has no right to collect income taxes, property taxes, or other fees because the right to do so is not spelled out in the U.S. Constitution.

The most radical believe that George Bush's "new world order" has come to pass and that the United Nations really runs the U.S. government. Some believe that the government is building concentration camps for its own citizens.

Oklahoma City Bombing

Within months of the Waco tragedy, a government report sharply criticized the ATF for botching the raid. But even harsher words were directed at the federal government by militia groups who viewed Waco as a campaign to disarm Americans and deny them religious freedom. Two years to the day after the Waco raid, the United States suffered the deadliest act of terrorism in its history.

On April 19, 1995, at 9 A.M., a car bomb ripped a nine-story hole in the Alfred P. Murrah Federal Building in downtown Oklahoma City. The building housed local offices of the ATF, Secret Service, Social Security Administration, Veterans Affairs Bureau, and Drug Enforcement Administration, as well as a day-care center and other federal offices. The explosion from the twelve-hundred-pound bomb was felt miles away. Smoke

This photograph of the north side of the federal building in downtown Oklahoma City shows astonishing devastation left by the bomb blast. The blast left 168 people dead, including children and infants.

streamed across the skyline and glass and debris were spread over ten blocks. Windows in buildings within five blocks were blasted out. Hardest hit was the day-care center on the building's second floor, which was directly above the blast.

When the bomb went off, according to Associated Press reports, Carole Lawton, sixty-two, a secretary in the Department of Housing and Urban Development, was sitting at her desk on the seventh floor when "all of a sudden the windows blew in. It got real dark, and the ceiling just started coming down." She then heard 'the roar of the whole building crumbling,'"[13] The floors of the building caved in from top to bottom. The north face of the building was obliterated. Burning debris and burning cars littered the streets. Initial reports listed at least twenty deaths, including seventeen children in the day-care center. Hundreds were injured, three hundred were unaccounted for, and many more were trapped in the rubble. The bomb also left a crater in the street eight feet deep and thirty feet across.

People frantically searched for loved ones and dozens of parents climbed through the rubble searching for their children. Rescue workers and firefighters were in tears, frustrated at the slow process of finding the injured and dead. The final death toll rose to 168 people.

Two Men Are Arrested

Immediately after the blast, most Americans jumped to the conclusion that the explosion in Oklahoma City was the work of Middle East terrorists. Dozens of Arabs were rounded up by police and held for questioning. Two days later, however, federal officials announced that the perpetrator was not a foreign terrorist but a twenty-seven-year-old American, Timothy McVeigh.

In a mute tribute to the children and others who died in the Oklahoma City bomb blast, people have left a teddy bear, flowers, and ribbons on the fence that surrounds the damaged building.

Just ninety minutes after the explosion, local police had pulled McVeigh over in Perry, Oklahoma, for driving without license plates. McVeigh was also found to be carrying an illegal weapon. Police did not immediately connect McVeigh to the bombing, but jailed him because the judge who was to arraign him on the weapons charge was busy with a trial.

In 1995, Timothy McVeigh is led from the courthouse after being charged with the Oklahoma City bombing. McVeigh was convicted of the bombing and sentenced to death in 1997.

When the FBI offered a $2 million reward and flashed sketches of suspects over the news wires, officers in Perry realized that they were holding the prime suspect. Within hours, investigators raided a farm owned by McVeigh's brother in Decker, Michigan, where the Michigan Militia, a right-wing, antigovernment extremist group, was headquartered. Another suspect, Terry Nichols, surrendered forty-eight hours after the bombing.

Authorities said the suspects rented a truck in Junction City, Kansas, about 270 miles from Oklahoma City. The truck was packed with a homemade bomb and parked outside the Murrah Building. After the explosion, the axle from the truck was found two blocks away. Major auto parts are marked with identification numbers to prevent theft, and the axle number allowed authorities to trace the truck to McVeigh.

On June 2, 1997, McVeigh was convicted on eleven counts of murder and conspiracy and sentenced to die by lethal injection. In January 1998, a jury convicted Terry Nichols of conspiracy and manslaughter. He was sentenced to life in prison without parole.

Militias Gain Attention

Right-wing militias gained a lot of attention after the Oklahoma blast because convicted bomber Timothy McVeigh had connections to militias in Michigan and Arizona. However extreme their views might seem, at least one thousand people in one state—California—shared them enough to form thirty-five paramilitary militia units up and down the state in the two years following the bombing. Similar statistics were reported in other states. The militia cause is aided by the Internet which has allowed thousands of disaffected Americans a voice on hundreds of promilitia home pages on the World Wide Web.

Militia members collect weapons, ammunition, and war supplies. Most claim to be patriots and believe that the U.S. Constitution sanctions any means necessary to overthrow a tyrannical government. They share wild conspiracy theories of international bankers who have set up concentration camps in the United States, begun helicopter flyovers, and trained thousands of Hong Kong police and thugs from the Crips and Bloods drug gangs to carry out a coup. Soon, militias warn, traitors will activate their "shadow government"—the Federal Emergency Management Agency (FEMA)—and impose their New World Order through mass arrests of citizens. According to the *San Francisco Examiner,* some extremists even believe the CIA bombed the federal building in Oklahoma City to pin the blame on innocent militia members.

According to the magazine *National Catholic Reporter*, one in five militia groups has direct links to the white supremacist movement. Figures from the watchdog group Klanwatch, an arm of the Southern Poverty Law Center in Montgomery, Alabama, show that many Ku Klux Klan (KKK) members have transformed themselves into "patriots" by switching over to militia groups as the Klan continues to falter in attracting new members. According to the Center for Democratic Renewal, an Atlanta-based group tracking racism, "Racists have codified their language. Now instead of saying they hate blacks, they will speak out against government supported 'welfare mothers.'" A spokesperson added, "Hate group leaders that once spouted racist language, now emphasize more antigovernment rhetoric."[14]

Brian Levin, associate director of Klanwatch, says:

> The thing that connects these groups, at its most tame, is this paranoid distrust of the federal government and this fanatical obsession with weapons and explosives. I believe there's a significant amount of racism and anti-Semitism in these groups, but I think a lot of them are sugar-coating their connections. It's extremely disturbing.[15]

Going After Militias

The growth of militia groups and their illegal activities has created a huge

Janet Reno

Janet Reno became America's first female attorney general at a tumultuous time. She was no sooner sworn in on March 12, 1993, than events in Waco, Texas, commanded her attention. As attorney general, Reno was in charge of the FBI, ATF, and other federal law enforcement agencies.

Reno was the daughter of two investigative reporters in Miami. Her mother was a remarkable woman who built the family home with her own hands. Janet was the president of the women's student government at Cornell University. In 1963 she earned her law degree at Harvard, where she was one of sixteen women in a class of five hundred. In 1978 Reno became the first woman to head a Florida county prosecutor's office as the state attorney from Dade County. A strong advocate for children's rights, Reno pursued child support from delinquent fathers and established a drug court that guided young nonviolent offenders into counseling. Reno was reelected as state attorney four times before being appointed as the seventy-eighth attorney general by Bill Clinton.

Although she was strongly criticized for decisions she made in Waco, Reno accepted full responsibility for her actions, admitted her mistakes, and enjoyed general public approval.

Attorney General Janet Reno came under heavy fire for her handling of the storming of the Branch Davidian compound.

workload for law enforcement officers. According to a 1997 article in *U.S. News & World Report*, over nine hundred internal terrorist cases were opened in 1997, compared with one hundred in 1995. The article goes on to profile men who commit violent terrorist acts as loners who belong to a small group. Some are characterized as neo-Nazi skinheads. They leave pipe bombs at local businesses, turn on blacks or homosexuals, and direct sniper fire at police. "Another Oklahoma City could happen tomorrow," says Robert Blitzer, head of the FBI's terrorism section. "There are still a lot of people out there with a lot of potential for violence."[16]

Credible bomb threats arrive at government offices every two weeks, on average. Favorite targets are police stations and offices of the Internal Revenue Service (IRS), the FBI, and the ATF.

After the Oklahoma City bombing, federal and local law enforcement agencies cracked down in an organized effort to identify and infiltrate the most violent of the hundreds of armed militias and "patriot" groups nationwide. In some places antigovernment movements have split into small cells to prevent penetration. Violent loners are considered the most unpredictable.

To aid in the crackdown, according to *U.S. News & World Report*, Congress and the White House have nearly tripled the FBI's counterterrorism budget since 1994, allowing the bureau to add 350 new agents to domestic terrorism cases. Agents have seized huge arsenals filled with machine guns, booby traps, semiautomatic weapons, all sorts of explosives, and bomb-making materials. Federal prosecutors have brought hundreds of criminal charges against far-right extremists, including conspiracy to bomb federal buildings, stockpiling of illegal weapons, financial fraud, and bank robbery.

The Unabomber

While the 1990s saw a rise of terrorism from the right, a left-wing terrorist with beliefs anchored in the 1970s was also making news. In May 1998, Theodore J. Kaczynski (Ka-zin-ski), fifty-five, was sentenced in a California courtroom to four life sentences plus thirty years in prison or psychiatric hospitals.

Kaczynski was accused of killing three people and injuring twenty-nine with homemade bombs. They were mailed to people who worked in high-tech fields over a period of eighteen years. Because his early bombs were mailed to universities (un) and airlines (a), the FBI referred to him as the Unabomber. The first bomb went off at Northwestern University near Chicago in 1978, the last on April 24, 1995, when timber industry lobbyist Gilbert Murray was killed by a package bomb mailed to his office in Sacramento, California. Also targeted were advertising officials, applied science professors, and computer experts.

In 1995 the letter-bomb terrorist contacted officials with a claim that the killing would stop if his thirty-five-thousand-word diatribe against modern society were published in major newspapers. In September 1995 the *New York Times* and the *Washington Post* jointly printed the manifesto, insisting that the action could save lives. The

Unabomber Ted Kaczynski was convicted of killing three people and injuring twenty-nine with his homemade letter bombs.

Unabomber's convoluted statement defined "the positive ideal" as nature:

> That is, WILD nature: those aspects of the functioning of the Earth and its living things that are independent of human management and free of human interference and control. And with wild nature we include human nature, by which we mean those aspects of the functioning of the human individual that are not subject to regulation by organized society but are products of chance, or free will, or God (depending on your religious or philosophical opinions).[17]

The bombing stopped, but David Kaczynski, forty-six, read the manifesto and was prompted to look through some of his brother Ted's long-forgotten papers. Struck by similarities between Ted's writings, which condemned technology for ruining the earth, and the Unabomber's, David called the FBI. Thanks to David Kaczynski's tip, the FBI—after eighteen years and two hundred suspects, in what was one of the longest and most expensive manhunts in history—finally traced the mail bombs to Ted Kaczynski in April 1996.

Closing the Book on the Unabomber

Agents dressed as lumberjacks and outdoor enthusiasts closed in on Kaczynski's Montana wilderness cabin after a month-long stakeout. The accused was charged with possession of an unregistered firearm after a search of his one-room shack yielded a partial pipe bomb. Investigators also found ten three-ring binders filled with bomb-making notes, as well as chemicals, tools, and metals that could be used in explosives. This was enough evidence to jail Kaczynski while the FBI put together a case.

Kaczynski, born and raised in a suburb of Chicago, was a brainy student who graduated from Harvard in 1962 and went on to earn master's and doctoral degrees from the University of Michigan. He spent two years as an assistant professor of mathematics at the University of California at Berkeley.

Kaczynski had few close personal relationships. He bought land in Montana in 1971 and built himself a plywood cabin on the Stemple Pass, on the Rocky Mountain Continental Divide near Lincoln (population one thousand). Neighbors describe him as a quiet, friendly, back-to-the-land eccentric who only emerged from his cabin to buy provisions or take out library books. Kaczynski had no car; he made his way around on an old bicycle fitted with snow chains. He had neither electricity nor running water at his secluded perch and grew much of his own food.

Kaczynski's family pleaded with the court at his trial to spare Ted the death penalty. Doctors testified that the Unabomber had a serious mental disorder that made him distrustful and violent. But Kaczynski insisted he was not mentally ill and fired his attorneys to keep them from portraying him as sick. Ultimately, in a bargain in which he admitted his guilt in court, Kaczynski was spared the death penalty.

"Going Postal"

There were common threads that tied together the tragedy at the Alfred P. Murrah Federal Building in Oklahoma and many Unabomber victims. Those killed or injured were at work. And these attacks were done by anonymous men bent on killing strangers. But another equally disturbing trend of violence at work emerged in the 1990s.

In 1998 alone, a postal worker in Elmira, New York, was arrested when he brought a rocket launcher to work and threatened coworkers. In Inglewood, California, two Department of Agriculture employees were slain by a coworker during a meeting to discuss work schedules. In Orange, California, a worker at the Caltrans yard killed four with an assault rifle. Even in the Vatican, a workplace-related homicide was carried out by a disgruntled soldier against the commander of the pope's Swiss Guard. The commander's wife was also shot.

These murders put a new term into widespread use. People were sardonically said to be "going postal" when they went to work and started shooting. The term was coined in 1986 when letter carrier Patrick Henry Sherrill, forty-

Rules for Firing Employees

With an increase in workplace violence, large companies devised guidelines for terminating employees in the 1990s. The following were compiled from internal company memos by Michael Moore in his book *Downsize This!*

Termination Guidelines

1. The termination meeting should last no more than 5 or 10 minutes. . . .
3. Avoid small talk. Get to the point. Don't debate. Don't discuss any issues of fairness. . . .
5. Have Kleenex available. . . .
9. Try not to make light of the situation by making jokes or trying to be funny. . . .
12. The following are the four most common emotional responses employees have upon learning of their termination. . . .

Anger. The louder the downsized employee talks, the softer the manager should talk. . . .

Denial. Just because a person has been told "you're fired," does not mean that he or she really hears it. . . .

Depression. This type of emotion should send an immediate warning signal. The person should be referred to a human resources counselor.

Hysteria. Both men and women are capable of overreacting to news of their termination. For terminated people who begin to cry after hearing the news, have a glass of water handy. . . .

14. Managers need to recognize the following symptoms during the meeting that may indicate the terminated worker could turn violent: expressions of unusual or bizarre thoughts; a fixation on weapons; romantic obsession; depression; and chemical dependence.

four, went on a rampage in Edmond, Oklahoma, gunning down fourteen coworkers and injuring six. Post offices were the site of at least thirty-six deaths over the next thirteen years.

Like airline accidents, incidents of workers going postal are relatively rare. But like airplane crashes, they always make front-page news. And the statistics are alarming. U.S. adults are eight to twenty times more likely to murder with guns than adults in other Western countries. By 1998 murder surpassed machine-related injuries as the second leading cause of occupational death in the United States, after car and truck accidents. Between 1992 and 1998, about one thousand Americans lost their lives in violent incidents at work. (It should be noted that only 10 percent involved employees who turned against coworkers.)

Still, mindful of public concern, government agencies and private companies began training managers to spot troubled workers and defuse workplace tensions before violence erupted. Managers tried to identify potential troublemakers by looking for certain characteristics of high risk, including men in their midthirties with a history of violence, weapons possession, substance abuse, or psychosis.

Violence in America

The murder rate in the United States in the 1990s topped forty thousand a year. Most victims die by gunfire and most know their murderers. But rare acts such as the Oklahoma City bombing make headlines because of their senselessness and randomness. And security experts agree, there is almost no way to stop a terrorist who is bent on random destruction.

The 1990s saw a rise in organized armed resistance to the laws of the United States. Militias were aided by the Internet and their fanatical ideas reached a larger audience than ever, including young people, whose increasing tendency toward violence has been portrayed as a most unwelcome trend in the 1990s.

Chapter Four

Children participate in a common 1990s education phenomenon: using a computer to learn their lessons.

Trends in Family and Education

For much of the 1990s, the United States was blessed with a strong economy. Jobs were plentiful, unemployment numbers were at historic lows, and consumer goods were cheap and plentiful. This was good news for American families, for whom economic issues are of vital importance.

As in every decade, the 1990s American family faced changes, challenges, and pressures. Trends that began in the late 1970s and 1980s continued to accelerate. The proportion of nuclear families—defined as two parents living with their children—continued to decline. More and more kids were raised by stepparents and even grandparents. The so-called Generation X—born after the post–World War II baby boomers—began families of their own. Some gay men and lesbians chose to adopt or have children. And in some instances traditional gender roles were reversed as mothers went to work while house husbands stayed home to raise the kids.

While politicians, preachers, and the media talked about "family values," the very definition of family stirred heated debate.

Changes in the Nuclear Family

Between 1965 and 1995, the divorce rate in the United States tripled, as did the percentage of children living in single-parent families. At the same time, children born out of wedlock also tripled; the illegitimacy rate in 1998 was 68 percent among African Americans and 22 percent among whites. Some blamed these trends for increases in youth violence, drug abuse, delinquency, depression, and suicide. Others countered that single parents can be just as capable of raising children as traditional families.

Statistics revealed, however, that children in single-parent families were six times more likely to be poor and three times more likely to have emotional or behavioral problems than children in two-parent families. Among those children, the rates of high school dropouts, teenage pregnancy, and drug abuse were much higher as well.

A single mother and her daughter enjoy a book. Out-of-wedlock births tripled between 1965 and 1995.

To help ease these problems, some advocated public policy changes that lessened the harmful economic effects of divorce on women and children. They also encouraged equal pay for women, flexible work schedules, and stripping away barriers that prevented women from reaching high-level executive positions.

In response to criticism that modern "no-fault" divorce laws make it too easy for a couple to split up, some state legislatures passed laws making it more difficult for people with children to get divorced.

Deadbeat Parents

The Clinton administration and the Congress took aim at so-called deadbeat dads (around 5 percent of whom are actually deadbeat moms) by passing a bill to collect money owed for child support. The bill was necessary because the scope of nonpayment was vast—deadbeat parents owed a cumulative $34 billion to 17 million children. The new federal provisions required states to revoke driver's, professional, and even fishing licenses for nonpayment. The law also allowed state governments to confiscate federal tax refunds and cross state lines to seize property.

Until the bill was signed, the Department of Health and Human Services used fifty-four local agencies and spent over $1.5 billion hunting down deadbeats. But the programs could not keep up with demand. The new laws allowed collection agencies to track down the money. Sometimes the collectors shamed the nonpaying parent, plastering his neighborhood with wanted posters, or in one case posting his name on a highway billboard. The ultimate penalty for nonpayment was jail time.

Good News and Bad About Teenage Pregnancy

Teen pregnancy was still a problem in the 1990s. In 1998 the bad news was that in the United States 1,402 babies were born every day to teenage mothers. The good news was that those numbers were down from the 1980s, following a trend that began in 1991.

According to *Newsweek* magazine, teenage pregnancy rates fell 11.9 percent from 1991 to 1998 due to increased use of contraceptives and sexual abstinence. Children of teenage mothers tend to be less healthy and smaller than those born to older mothers, and in turn have higher rates of teenage pregnancy and delinquency themselves.

Experts calculated that the problem cost the country about $7 billion a year in lost taxes, public assistance dollars, and criminal justice costs. To counteract these negative effects, many programs focused on discouraging teenage pregnancy.

Women's health organizations such as Planned Parenthood and religious and social conservatives both believed education was key, but they differed on what to teach: Planned Parenthood believed in talking about safe sex and contraceptives, while conservatives believed in abstinence-only programs. Both groups' messages might have contributed to the reversal in a long-growing problem.

A teenage mother holds her toddler son. Teenage pregnancy rates began to fall in the 1990s.

The falling teenage pregnancy rate of the 1990s cut across all racial, ethnic, and geographic lines. In fact, the pregnancy rate among African American teens, traditionally higher than white teens, was down by 21 percent, the lowest level ever reported. Government figures also show that the teen pregnancy rate among Hispanics, though still the highest in the nation, tumbled by 4.8 percent between 1995 and 1996.

In the past, drops in teen pregnancy rates were largely due to abortions, but the numbers of teen abortions also dropped in the nineties. According to the federal government, contraceptive use was up among teens. Dr. Robert Blum, director of adolescent health at the University of Minnesota, said:

> We're seeing more than a fourfold increase in the use of condoms. Fifteen

years ago only 11 percent of teens used condoms. Now it's 44 percent. And inner-city teenagers are increasingly using highly effective Depo-Provera injections or Norplant [a long-lasting contraceptive implant].[18]

But contraception did not account for the entire trend. Many more teens than in the past were simply choosing not to have sex. According to Isabel Sawhill, president of the National Campaign to Prevent Teen Pregnancy:

> My sense is that more kids realize it's OK not to have sex—that, in fact, it may even be cool. We seem to have succeeded in convincing teens that delaying sex may be a better idea, because more are [waiting until they are older].[19]

A nineties trend showed a growing number of schools across the country forming "virgin clubs," with members publicly pledging not to have sex.

Although the news was encouraging, pregnancy researchers did not declare victory. The United States still led Western nations in the rate of teen pregnancy. Four out of ten American teens—nearly a million every year—become pregnant at least once before they turn twenty, and 80 percent are unmarried.

Grandparents Raising Kids

Another growing trend of the 1990s was grandparents raising their grandchildren. A 1997 study by University of California, Berkeley, and the University of Toronto showed about 11 percent of the grandparents studied were providing primary care for their grandchildren for a period of at least six months. Of that group, 20 percent had been caring for their grandchildren for ten years or more.

According to the U.S. census, the number of children who live with grandparents with no parent present jumped sharply between 1989 and 1995, from 882,000 to 1.46 million.

The study describes the typical caregiver as a married white woman, just under sixty, who lives with her husband and her grandchildren in an urban area. The median household income is about $22,000 a year. About 23 percent of the caregivers studied live below the poverty line while caring for their grandchildren.

The reasons for the growing trend were substance abuse by an adult son or daughter, followed by child abuse and neglect, teenage pregnancy, and divorce. While grandparents raising grandkids has always been more common in lower-income, inner-city neighborhoods, in the nineties more middle- and upper-class grandparents began to raise their children's children, especially those who have lost an adult child to one addiction or another.

While the median age of grandparent caregivers was fifty-seven, thirty-six thousand were over the age of seventy-five.

Trends in Schooling

The emotional problems caused by divorce and teen pregnancy reverberated in schools across the nation, deepening the mood of controversy and crisis reigning in public education in the 1990s.

At a time when many entry-level jobs required college-level skills, American primary and secondary education was found to be lacking. A middecade study showed that a full 47 percent of twenty-one- to twenty-five-year-olds could not use a calculator to determine a price discount. The test also showed that literacy skills of these college-age people were 11 to 14 percent lower than a matched group tested in 1985. Former secretary of education Richard Riley warned:

> Ninety million adults in this country do not have the literacy skills they need to function in our increasingly complex education system.[20]

Lower test scores, discipline problems, and widespread distrust of school bureaucracy put schools in the center of heated political debates about how to fix America's public education system. Some wanted to institute school vouchers that would grant parents tax incentives to send their children to private and parochial schools. Others stressed more funding for books and classrooms, and stronger efforts to shrink class sizes. People on all sides of the issue clamored for more and more stringent student—and teacher—testing.

In response to dropping test scores, President Clinton advocated networking classrooms around the country by hooking them up to the Internet.

An explosion in test taking that began in the 1970s continued to grow—and cost more. The National Education Association (NEA) estimates that American schools spent $700 to $900 million in 1994 on testing alone.

President Clinton supported the idea that computers are necessary to improve education. In 1997, he announced a plan to link every U.S. classroom to the Internet by the year 2000. The federal government further promised $2 billion for high-tech classrooms, and Clinton exhorted corporate America to help pay for the computers, signing a bill that required high-tech companies to help schools get computer services at low prices.

Another 1990s problem in public education resulted from an unforeseen baby boom first observed in 1995. A growing population and a large influx of immigrants were causing severe overcrowding in some U.S. elementary schools. Kindergarten enrollment alone rose 22 percent from 1980 to 1993. Districts that demolished unused schools in the early 1980s were left scrambling to find classroom space. By 1995, 6 million more children were attending school than were ten years earlier. High school populations were also growing sharply, with an expected increase of 13 percent

Students Want More Challenges

A study by the Public Agenda Foundation asked teenagers what they wanted from schools, and a majority of black, white, and Hispanic students said that they were not challenged enough in public schools. According to *Forbes* magazine, the remarkable 1997 study, called "Getting By: What American Teenagers Really Think About Their Schools," used a combination of polling and focus groups to answer that question.

The study concluded that a majority of American teens wanted higher academic and behavioral standards in their schools. Students of all racial groups said that schools expected little of them and they responded by doing just enough to get by. The great majority said they wanted a well-disciplined and orderly environment for learning. Seven out of ten said there were too many disruptive youngsters in their classes. And 82 percent said that the troublemakers should be removed from regular classes so that others can learn.

Half the teenagers said that too many students got away with being late and not doing their work. The same number said that their schools didn't challenge them to do their best. Self-esteem was also important to the students surveyed. Close to 90 percent believed that "feeling good about themselves" would help them do better in school, and that it was more important than completing their schoolwork.

between 1997 and 2007, which will require about 150,000 more teachers.

School Uniforms

In the 1990s, school districts coast to coast resurrected a policy to help reduce discipline problems: Children in at least thirty-five cities began to wear uniforms to school. The trend started in 1995, when California's Long Beach School District, subject to intractable discipline and gang problems, became the nation's first school district to require students to wear uniforms. A year later, there was a 50 percent drop in the number of weapons found in school and the number of fights also declined 50 percent. Uniforms were said to reduce arguments over whose sneakers cost more and who wore the best designer clothes.

All over the country, uniforms were said to combat disorder and academic underachievement. Jeans, sweatshirts, and team jackets were banned in favor of tidier attire.

Clinton supported the movement toward school uniforms in a January 1996 radio address:

> If it means that the schoolrooms will be more orderly, more disciplined . . . and that our young people will learn to evaluate themselves by what they are on the inside instead of what they're wearing on the outside, then our public schools should be able to require their students to wear school uniforms.[21]

Uniforms appealed to parents for their low cost, about one hundred dollars. "Uniforms are considerably less expensive than the name-brand clothes that most of our children want,"[22] said a mother in Salinas, California.

In 1998 the New York City school board voted to require elementary school students to wear uniforms. New York City is the nation's largest school system; the decision affected a half-million children.

Violence at School

While most schools were relatively safe places, a few high-profile schoolyard massacres shocked America in the late 1990s. The first incident occurred in the small town of Pearl, Mississippi, on October 2, 1997, when Luke Woodham, sixteen, stabbed his mother to death, then went to school and shot nine of his classmates, killing two.

Then in December 1997, in the small, conservative town of Paducah, Kentucky, Michael Carneal, fourteen, pulled out a semiautomatic rifle from his backpack and fired off twelve shots, killing three students and wounding five. The students Carneal shot were among a group of thirty-five assembled for a prayer group. People were doubly

Fourteen-year-old Michael Carneal opened fire on his fellow classmates at his high school in Paducah, Kentucky. In the shooting, three students were killed and five others were injured.

shocked because Carneal was a B student who played in the band and stayed out of trouble at school, save for two minor infractions.

In what seemed to be a rash of copycat crimes, a wave of schoolyard shootings swept through small-town America. James Fox, dean of criminal justice at Northeastern University, states:

> A decade ago, the idea of shooting up a schoolyard wouldn't cross anyone's mind. Now young people have prior examples. These kids probably couldn't spell Paducah . . . but they'd heard of it.[23]

The small number of murders committed by children under fourteen has barely budged in twenty years, Fox points out, but among older teens the rate has doubled in a dozen years.

The next incident was a well-planned ambush at Westside Middle

School in Jonesboro, Arkansas, in May 1998. Mitchell Johnson and Andrew Golden, ages eleven and thirteen, assembled a massive quantity of weapons and ruthlessly shot fifteen people in less than a minute, killing four students and a teacher and mother of a two-year-old son who died trying to protect a child. All of the victims were females.

The trend continued in May 1998 when a young man with an obsession with guns and bombs walked into a crowded cafeteria at Thurston High School in Springfield, Oregon, shortly before 8 A.M. Within a minute or less, Kipland Kinkel fired fifty rounds from a semiautomatic rifle. Twenty-four students were wounded, two of them fatally.

Experts blame everything from access to guns to violent video games and television for the trend. But they also warn that students who are prone to violence usually state their intentions before they act, and might be diverted from killing if parents and teachers simply paid more attention to what they say. According to University of Virginia psychologist Dewey Cornell:

> Many kids give clear indications . . . but they aren't taken seriously. We need to take violence threats as seriously as we take threats of suicide.[24]

The funeral of Shannon Wright, the teacher killed when two boys aged eleven and thirteen ruthlessly opened fire at their middle school. In addition to Wright, four students were killed.

The good news is that, like adult homicide, the number of killings by those seventeen or younger had actually declined by nearly a third since the early 1990s. A 1998 report from the U.S. Department of Education showed that violence was still rare in the nation's schools. Among the 1,234 elementary and secondary schools surveyed for the report, 43 percent reported no crimes at all during the 1996–1997 school year. Most school-related offenses were catalogued as minor incidents such as theft, vandalism, or fights without weapons. Gunplay at schools in the 1990s continued to kill twenty to thirty youths a year. But research showed that weapons-related violence in schools was no higher than in the 1970s.

Fifteen-year-old Kipland Kinkel killed two students and injured twenty-four when he opened fire with a semiautomatic rifle at his high school in Springfield, Oregon.

Statistics also show that 90 percent of children under seventeen who were murdered were killed by adults. And schools were actually rated as some of the safest places for children. For instance, fifteen thousand people were murdered in Los Angeles from 1990 to 1997. Only five were killed at school, in a school system that serves 2 million children every day.

Generation X Comes of Age

As the 1990s drew to a close, a new generation of Americans was coming into its own. Its members, born between 1963 and 1977, were dubbed "Generation X," "Gen X," or "Xers" by the media. The term became the often-loathed namesake of some 50 million Americans. They had long been overshadowed—and outnumbered—by the baby boomers in the White House, on Wall Street, and in the boardrooms.

Time magazine elaborated the media stereotype about Gen Xers:

> Beavis and Butt-head were their icons; Beck's "Loser" was their song ("Savin' all your food stamps and burnin' down the trailer park"); Richard Linklater's *Slacker,* with its Austin, Texas, deadbeats, was their movie. This was the MTV generation: Net surfing, nihilistic . . . piercers whining about McJobs; latchkey legacies, fearful of commitment. Passive and powerless, they were content, it seemed, to party on in a Wayne's Netherworld, one with more anti-heroes—Kurt Cobain, Dennis Rodman, the Menendez brothers—than role models. The label that stuck was from Douglas Coupland's 1991 novel, *Generation X*, a tale of languid youths musing over "mental ground zero—the location where one visualizes oneself during the dropping of the atomic bomb: frequently a shopping mall."[25]

However, surveys indicated that the Xers were founding small businesses, starting high-tech companies, and making movies in and out of Hollywood. A 1993 University of Michigan study found that twenty-five- to thirty-

Higher Education in the Nineties

While public education was under fire from all sides in the 1990s, the cost of a college education continued to accelerate dramatically. Between 1992 and 1998, college tuition costs climbed an average of 5 percent a year. This rate increase was three times greater than inflation. In 1997 alone, the increase added between $136 and $670 per year to tuition costs, making $3,000 the norm for public schools. Costs at private colleges average about $13,000 per year.

When room and board expenses were factored in, total college costs reached about $10,000 a year for public and $21,400 for private institutions. College officials blamed the rate hikes on cuts in federal funding and increased operating costs. But critics claim extravagance has also contributed to the problem—especially in the salaries of administrators. Faced with mounting pressure from parents, a congressional committee began looking into the issue.

four-year-olds were starting businesses at three times the rate of thirty-five- to fifty-five-year-olds. Xers worked 3.6 percent longer each week than the national average, and were better educated and more grassroots oriented than their older counterparts. And they appeared to have a well-developed social consciousness.

A 1997 study by Infocus found that 42 percent of adults ages eighteen to thirty-four tried a new product because they felt the product, its packaging, or the manufacturer benefited the environment; 51 percent switched brands because of environmental concerns. Independent Sector, a Washington-based research group, found that 38 percent of eighteen- to twenty-four-year-olds volunteered within the past year, along with more than half the twenty-five- to thirty-three-year-olds.

The main hallmark of the X generation seemed to be its diversity. In the book *The Fourth Turning*, a study of generational change, historians William Strauss and Neil Howe write:

> Compared to any other generation born in this century, theirs is less cohesive, its experiences wider, its ethnicity more polyglot and its culture more splintery. Today's young adults define themselves by sheer divergence.[26]

Generation X grew up in a world created by baby boomers. They inherited benefits as well as drawbacks. But as the twenty-first century dawned, and the baby boomers began to retire, a new generation, with a new set of problems, talents, and expectations, was poised to take over the reins of power.

Chapter Five

Police were out in full force after riots in South Central Los Angeles. During the 1990s, the racial divide seemed to grow wider.

Gender and Race Conflict

Among the most rapid and dramatic changes in the United States in the 1990s was the shift in the ethnic makeup of American citizens. The population of the country increased by 25 million people during the decade; more than a million a year were immigrants. Most of these immigrants came from Latin America, the Caribbean, and Asia.

In 1993, *Time* magazine dubbed Miami, Florida, the capital of Latin America. At that time more than 60 percent of Miami's citizens spoke Spanish at home. On the West Coast, the Los Angeles school district taught students who spoke one or more of eighty-two different languages.

Asian Americans made up another growing segment of the population. In

1995 the freshman class at the University of California, Los Angeles (UCLA), was 42 percent Asian American; Asian Americans made up 33 percent of the students at UC Berkeley.

A moderate anti-immigrant backlash ensued. A few states passed resolutions making English the official language for state business. In 1998 voters in California passed Proposition 227, which overhauled the existing bilingual education program in favor of English immersion classes for nonfluent students.

As America neared the twenty-first century, the balance between honoring differences and learning to work together was a matter of debate. There were violent racial flare-ups and emotional gender conflicts. Several well-publicized episodes showed that America had a long list of social problems to solve.

Clarence Thomas and Anita Hill

In 1991, the televised hearings for the Clarence Thomas nomination to the Supreme Court put the spotlight on

Shifting Religious Loyalties

By the 1990s, the United States had become the most religiously diverse country in the world. At least two hundred denominations existed, with new entities appearing every year. This trend was brought about by immigration, intermarriage, and displeasure with old-line religions.

In 1998 the United States was home to 4 million Muslims, five times as many as there were in 1970. Close to half of them were African Americans, many of whom were born into other religions. The number of Muslims was expected to soon overtake the number of Jews, whose numbers remained at about 5.5 million.

Two million Americans identified themselves as Buddhists, a tenfold increase since 1970. The number of Hindus grew from 100,000 to 950,000 in the same period, Sikhs from 1,000 to 200,000.

While 85 percent of Americans were Christians in 1998, the face of Christianity was changing. In the last quarter of the twentieth century, the fastest growing religious communities were Pentecostal, Mormon, and Jehovah's Witnesses. Roman Catholics had 60 million adherents, 30 percent of whom were Latinos. At the same time the Southern Baptist Convention, the country's second-largest denomination with 16 million members, had seen its ethnic membership grow by 50 percent, particularly among Asians and Latinos.

Perhaps the most telling figure of America's religious transformation was that by 1998, half of all Americans died as members of a different denomination than they were born into.

sexual harassment in the workplace and potentially deep divisions between genders.

During the Reagan years, the Supreme Court had moved steadily to the right. The liberal wing of the court was growing old and ill. In 1991 the Court's most liberal judge, Thurgood Marshall, eighty-three—the first and only African American on the Court—announced his retirement. Bush quickly nominated a young black judge with strong conservative beliefs. When Clarence Thomas came before the Democratic-controlled Senate, he stirred up a political storm over race and the rightward movement of the court. But in the end, it was a story told by Anita Faye Hill—a woman who had previously worked for Thomas—that captured the country's attention.

Hill, who had been Thomas's personal assistant when he headed the Equal Employment Opportunity Commission

Law professor Anita Hill (above) testifies before a Senate Judiciary Committee that she was sexually harassed by Supreme Court nominee Clarence Thomas (right) while she was employed by him. The televised hearings fascinated viewers.

(EEOC), told her televised story before the Senate Judiciary Committee. She described a pattern of sexual harassment in which Thomas made suggestive comments and advances that she felt powerless to stop. There was X-rated testimony about Thomas watching pornographic movies, uttering obscene and embarrassing phrases, and grabbing women inappropriately. Thomas denied all charges.

On October 15, 1991, after great national controversy, Thomas was confirmed on a 52-48 vote by the full Senate. He has since proven himself one of the Court's most staunchly conservative justices. The allegations against him laid bare a gulf in male-female relations in Washington, where the corridors of power have always been dominated by men, and in workplaces throughout the country, where issues of parity and harassment continue to be debated. The harsh questioning of Anita Hill before the all-male panel of senators galvanized women voters, who in 1992 elected a record number of female candidates for Congress, leading reporters to call the election "The Year of the Woman." After the Thomas-Hill hearings, complaints of sexual harassment in the workplace skyrocketed. The Anita Hill episode was given credit for this trend.

The Mitsubishi Sexual Harassment Case

In June 1998 a record $34 million was awarded to female workers at the Mitsubishi Motors factory in Normal, Illinois. In exchange for abandoning a two-year fight against the Equal Employment Opportunity Commission (EEOC), the largest settlement of a corporate case ever was paid out to 350 women who claimed they were sexually harassed on the job. The deal also obligated the 636-acre car assembly plant to be supervised by outside monitors. Although company officials steadfastly denied the charges, they agreed to the settlement.

The harassment of female employees was detailed in a lawsuit filed in April 1996. Female assembly-line workers told of being fondled, targeted with air guns, and taunted with obscene names. Some females claimed they were propositioned by male workers, managers, and even union officials to provide sexual services.

Although the Mitsubishi settlement was the biggest ever in a sexual harassment case, other discrimination suits have brought even larger sums. In 1992 a group of female employees won $250 million from State Farm Insurance for denying them jobs as sales agents.

The Rodney King Beating

Race remained one of America's most explosive issues and continued to be one of the most difficult and delicate matters to discuss in the 1990s.

No one watching television in March 1991 could escape the repeated showing of a videotape in which motorist Rodney King was brutally clubbed by officers of the Los Angeles Police Department (LAPD). On March 3, King and two friends were speeding on a Los Angeles freeway in a white Hyundai that King had used to rob a grocery store sixteen months earlier. King, who had recently been paroled from prison for armed robbery and assault, panicked when he heard police sirens behind him.

King tried to elude California Highway Patrol (CHP) officers at speeds up to one hundred miles per hour. The high-speed chase was quickly joined by a caravan of LAPD patrol cars, two security officers from the LA school district, and a police helicopter. King was finally forced off the road near a complex of apartment buildings. By this time, a total of twenty-three LAPD officers, two CHP officers, and two security guards were chasing the Hyundai.

At some point, the officers began clubbing King with their nightsticks. As the confrontation got noisier, a crowd of people gathered nearby. One of the people in the crowd was George Holliday, thirty-three, who grabbed his video camera and began to film the unfolding drama.

What Holliday saw through the lens was a large black man cordoned off by police officers who had pushed the man to the ground. While one officer shot darts from his taser stun gun, three others used their batons to beat King all over his body. They kicked and stomped King, shot him with an electric harpoon, dragged him around by

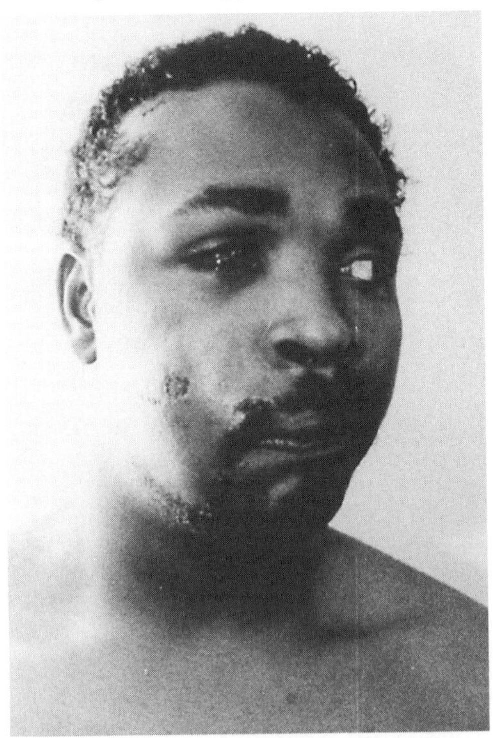

The bruised and battered face of Rodney King after a high-speed chase to avoid officers of the California Highway Patrol resulted in King's severe beating. The videotape of King's beating was shown hundreds of times on television.

the long wires, tied his hands and feet together, and shouted racial epithets.

In the eighty-one-second video, King can be seen getting up on his hands and knees twice, covering his face for protection, and trying to escape the assault. The camera also recorded a group of police officers passively watching—but not attempting to stop—the beating. When the tape was later played in slow motion, observers were able to count fifty-six blows and six kicks. After King was handcuffed and dragged on his stomach to wait for an ambulance, four officers made jokes about the assault. Even after King was taken to the hospital, a nurse overheard one of the officers taunting King and joking about the beating.

After the assault, Sergeant Stacey Koon sent a message back to his watch commander: "U [patrol unit] just had a big time use of force—tased and beat the suspect of CHP pursuit, Big Time." The commander responded, "Oh well, I'm sure the lizard didn't deserve it—Ha, Ha."[27]

On examination, doctors found King had sustained a fractured eye socket, a broken cheekbone, a broken leg, facial nerve damage, a severe concussion, bruises all over his body, and burns from the taser stun gun. The blows had broken his skull in eleven places and knocked the fillings out of several of his teeth. King was quickly stitched up and transferred to a medical jail ward.

Tests later showed King was probably legally intoxicated at the time of the chase, and he had traces of marijuana in his blood. He was booked for evading arrest and held in jail for four days. He was released when prosecutors claimed they did not have enough evidence to jail him. Doctors finally operated on his broken bones eleven days after the beating.

Outrage and Reaction

The day after the beating, Holliday went to the local police station to file a report about the assault. He was treated politely but no action was taken. Holliday decided to pursue justice on his own and took his tape to Los Angeles TV station KTLA, which aired the sensational footage. Picked up by CNN later that evening, beamed around the globe by satellite, the King beating held the public's attention across the country.

The reaction to the tape was immediate and intense. Politicians from President George Bush to civil rights leader Jesse Jackson decried the use of police violence against an unarmed black man. Many could not believe that such a beating could still take place in the United States in the 1990s. California assemblyman Curtis R. Tucker said,

"When black people in Los Angles see a police car approaching, they don't know whether justice will be meted out or whether judge, jury, and executioner is pulling up behind them."[28]

Less than two weeks after the beating, a grand jury indicted LAPD officers Stacey Koon, Laurence Powell, Ted Briseno, and Timothy Wind for unlawful assault and use of excessive force. Because of the publicity caused by the tape, the trial was moved out of Los Angeles to the conservative, predominantly white suburb of Simi Valley. In February 1992, Simi Valley was the center of national and international fame as the site of the *People v. Powell et al.*, or the Rodney King beating trial.

The defense, representing the police, emphasized King's background as an aggressive convicted felon who had tested positive for alcohol and marijuana and threatened the arresting officers.

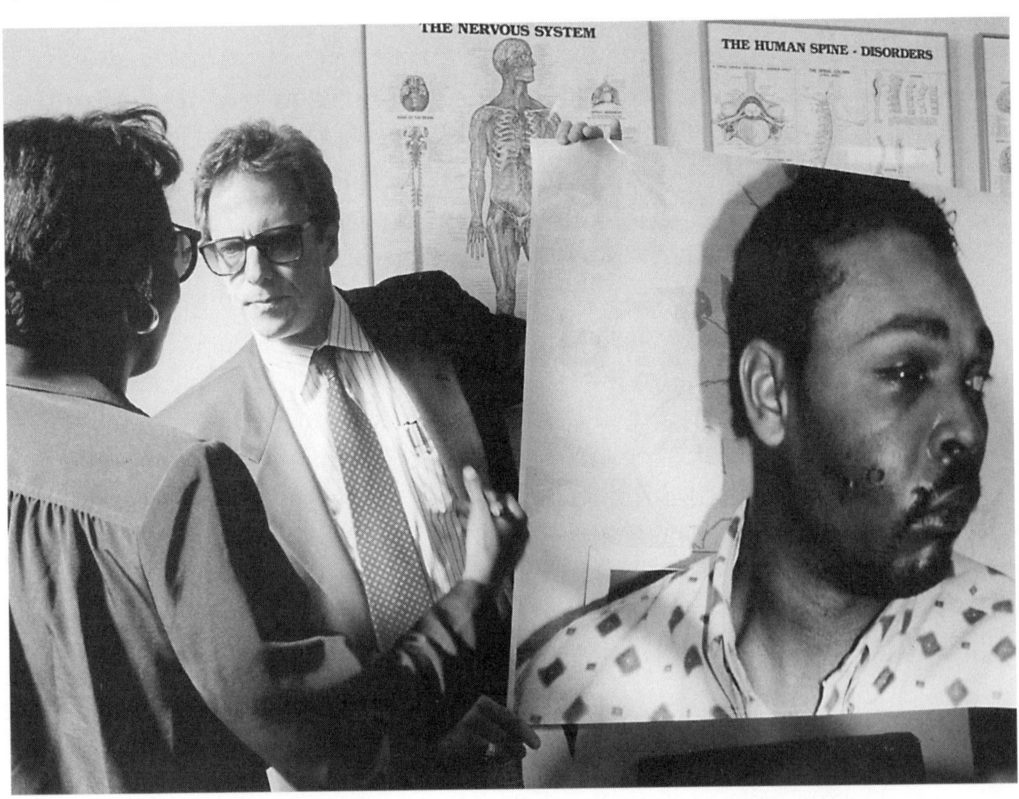

Lawyer Steven Lerman (center) holds a photo of Rodney King while speaking with reporters about the civil case he was about to file on behalf of King. The acquittal of the officers resulted in mass rioting in Los Angeles.

On April 29, 1992, after six weeks of testimony and six hours of deliberation the jury acquitted the officers on all counts. Legal columnist Marcia Chambers wrote about the verdict, "It is always difficult to convict a cop, especially in the suburbs. . . . The prosecutor found out that in Simi Valley, at least, there is no such thing as a smoking gun."[29] Even Bush was shocked by the verdict. He said the trial's outcome "has left us all with a deep sense of personal frustration and anguish."[30]

Outside the courtroom, hundreds of reporters from across the globe reported the news. The verdict was met with stunned disbelief by many. Meanwhile, pent-up rage in the black community smoldered and finally exploded late that afternoon on the corner of Florence and Normandie in South Central Los Angeles.

The LA Riots

In the 1990s, Los Angeles was the most culturally diverse urban area in the United States. South Central was the heart of African American Los Angeles. It had been a magnet for black immigrants from Texas and Louisiana since the turn of the century. By the late 1990s the community was home to 3 million people, nearly half of whom were immigrants from Mexico and Latin America.

Most residents of South Central can remember vividly where they were when they first heard the not-guilty verdict in the King case. Rev. Cecil L. Murray, pastor of the First African Methodist Episcopal Church, writes:

> When the verdicts were announced, I was . . . in the church looking at television with about two hundred others. . . . I just found the tears flowing—I guess I just cried out of sixty-four years of utter frustration and hope. . . . Then we stood in a circle and had a word of prayer.[31]

Rev. Kenneth Flowers of the Messiah Baptist Church had a different reaction. He said, "They're gonna burn this city down!"[32]

The crowd at Florence and Normandie mushroomed as people rushed out of their homes and apartments, some bewildered, some angry, some in a state of shock. Blacks, Latinos, young, old, men, women, and workers began to mill around in the street. At 4 P.M. the crowd began throwing rocks and bottles. People in cars tried to navigate the narrow passage left in the middle of the street. Some were dragged from their cars and beaten.

Reginald Denny, a white truck driver, was on his way to warn a black friend about the impending violence. At a red light, he was pulled from his truck and viciously attacked by four young black men. One man repeatedly beat Denny on the head with a brick. Another stole his wallet. As cameras rolled on an overhead helicopter, millions of Americans watched the assault live on TV.

What followed was an orgy of arson and looting. For the next twenty-four hours, LAPD officers were virtually absent from the scene as 9 people were killed and 190 others were wounded. Hundreds of homes and businesses were burned and looted in the seven-by-fifteen-mile area of South Central. Adults and children hauled off bulging sacks of goods from toy stores, auto stores, and liquor stores. Sixty percent of the buildings damaged were owned or operated by Korean immigrants.

Relations between Korean merchants and their black customers had been tense for some time. In 1991, the wife of a Korean grocer fatally shot black teenager Latasha Harlins in the back after accusing her of stealing a bottle of orange juice. The incident was

Rioters run amok in South Central Los Angeles in protest of the acquittal of LAPD officers in the Rodney King beating.

caught on videotape by the store's security camera, and the tape was replayed on the news hundreds of times. Found guilty of manslaughter, the woman was only ordered to perform community service. The intense frustration over the verdict exploded into violence against all Korean merchants during the riots.

A National Guardsman holds looters in a makeshift prison made out of the gate that was meant to protect a local toy store. The riots left fifty-four dead and caused $1 billion in property damage.

The Cost of the Uprising

By the second day of the riots, over four thousand fires had consumed twenty-five blocks of South Central. Police with shotguns guarded firefighters who battled some of the blazes. Acrid smoke hung over the city. Rodney King himself appealed for peace: "People," he pleaded, "I just want to say . . . can't we all get along? I mean, we're all stuck here for a while. Let's try to work it out."[33]

LA police were criticized for not reacting to the violence. Police chief Daryl Gates was out of town, and the city had not organized a plan of action in case of a disturbance. Governor Pete Wilson ordered 750 patrol officers and 2,000 National Guardsmen to the scene. Bush called in federal troops. In all, over 10,000 officers and troops arrived to quell the riots.

By May 2, residents were cleaning up the debris from four days of the nation's worst rioting in the twentieth century. The riots left 54 dead, caused $1 billion in property damage, and destroyed at least 25,000 jobs. Rioters had destroyed over 3,800 buildings and vandalized, looted, and burned another 10,000.

In the months after the riots, controversial police chief Daryl Gates was forced to resign. His successor was Willie Williams, a well-respected African American police chief from Philadelphia. Several commissions were impaneled and recommended numerous changes within the culture of the LAPD to prevent another Rodney King–type incident. These changes included increased emphasis on

The Million Man March

In October 1995 African American men from all over the country went to Washington, D.C., for the Million Man March. The event was organized by Nation of Islam leader Louis Farrakhan. The men came to pledge an end to "black-on-black" violence, and to renew their commitment to women, children, family, and church—and to political activism. In spite of accusations against Farrakhan that he excluded women, promoted a separatist philosophy, and was anti-Semitic, he was able to mobilize and electrify the crowd.

Controversial black leader Louis Farrakhan gives an emotional speech during the Million Man March in Washington, D.C., on October 16, 1995.

African American men in the Million Man March wanted to defy the negative stereotypes many Americans held of black men. But the statistics fueling the stereotypes were powerful. At the time of the march, black men had a 1-in-24 chance of being murdered, a ratio six times higher than white Americans. The average life expectancy for an African American male was sixty-five, the age white males could expect to live to forty years earlier. Black men made up 6 percent of the population but 48 percent of the prison population. And 60 percent of black women who gave birth were single mothers.

The day's events, held on the Mall in Washington, included praying, singing, a flag-raising ceremony, and African dance presentations. Prominent African Americans from religion, government, business, health, education, and the arts gave speeches. When the men returned home they helped sponsor voter registration drives, food banks, and tuition programs. The marchers made a pledge: "I will strive to improve myself spiritually, morally, mentally, socially, politically, and economically for the benefit of myself, my family, and my people."

community policing and the institution of minority outreach programs. In a civil trial, King was awarded $3.8 million in damages for his injuries from the city of Los Angeles.

Koon and Powell, two of the four officers who beat King, were convicted in federal court of violating King's civil rights and sentenced to two and a half years in prison.

O.J. Simpson and Nicole Brown

Two years after the LA riots, another racially charged case in Los Angeles made headlines around the world. Orenthal James (O.J.) Simpson was a well-loved African American football hero from the housing projects of San Francisco. A Heisman Trophy winner, he had set several records during his football career with the Buffalo Bills and San Francisco 49ers and achieved success as an actor and celebrity pitchman after his retirement from the game.

Simpson married Nicole Brown, who was white, in 1985. During their turbulent marriage, Nicole called police at least eight times to report that O.J. beat her. Simpson received light penalties on the few occasions when he was arrested. In 1992 Nicole finally left O.J. and filed for divorce. She moved to a condominium in the Brentwood area of Los Angeles.

On the evening of June 12, 1994, Nicole dined at a local restaurant. After she got home, she remembered that she had left her glasses behind. Waiter Ron Goldman brought Nicole's glasses to her nearby condominium. Shortly after midnight, a couple walking by encountered a white dog with bloody paws. They followed the dog to the violently brutalized bodies of the murdered Nicole and Ron Goldman. Each had been stabbed repeatedly.

In what became known as the "trial of the century," football hero O.J. Simpson was tried for the murder of his ex-wife Nicole Brown and friend Ronald Goldman.

By June 17, the media were calling the murders the crime of the decade. O.J. Simpson was the main suspect. When he did not turn himself in voluntarily in response to a warrant, police discovered he and his friend Al Cowlings had fled in Simpson's white Ford Bronco. The police located the Bronco several hours later and several dozen CHP cars gave chase. Police and television helicopters recorded the scene from above as the white Bronco drove along the San Diego Freeway.

This may have been the most widely watched television event in history, as 95 million Americans (two-thirds of the country's households) were riveted for nearly two hours in front of their TV sets. Finally, the Bronco pulled into Simpson's Brentwood estate at 8 P.M. As the sun was setting, the fugitive Simpson surrendered to police without incident.

The Racial and Gender Divide

From the very beginning, blacks and whites viewed the O.J. Simpson affair differently. Interracial marriage was accepted but apparently still controversial for blacks and whites. W. C. Rhoden, writer at *Emerge* magazine, wrote: "The marriage [between O.J. and Nicole] has driven some blacks to fury: 'Why do so many successful black men have to marry white women? . . . If he had stayed with that black woman [O.J.'s first wife], he wouldn't be in all this trouble.'"[34]

There was also controversy over the way police allowed the car chase to go on for such a long time. A CNN-Gallup poll found that 43 percent of whites but only 23 percent of blacks felt Simpson had been treated "too leniently" on the day he was arrested.

Simpson was jailed awaiting trial, but he assembled a "dream team" of lawyers to see to his defense. His trial became an international media circus and made celebrities out of lawyers Johnnie Cochran and Marcia Clark and Judge Lance Ito. It lasted from September 26, 1994, to October 5, 1995, and was the first trial in American history to be given gavel-to-gavel coverage on TV and radio. It became a cable television institution, driving dozens of daily talk shows.

The mostly black jury saw 1,105 pieces of evidence and 45,000 pages of testimony. Although the evidence against O.J. seemed overwhelming, some of it was mishandled by police. Mark Fuhrman, a detective who had conducted much of the crime scene police work, was proved to have lied on the witness stand and to have racist beliefs. Convinced of the possibility of tampered evidence, the jury acquitted Simpson. He walked out of the courtroom a free man. TV cameras captured black people assembled in barbershops and restaurants cheering and clapping when the news was announced. White people were shown shaking their heads in disbelief.

When O.J. Simpson was acquitted in the murders of Nicole Brown and Ronald Goldman, opinion over the verdict split along racial lines, further demarcating the differences between black and white.

The verdict sharply divided black and white America. According to a *Newsweek* poll taken immediately after the trial, 85 percent of blacks agreed with the not guilty verdict and 80 percent thought the jury was fair. By contrast, only 32 percent of the whites agreed with the verdict, but 50 percent thought the jury was "fair and impartial."

The case also put spousal abuse in the headlines. White women were outraged that Simpson, an admitted wife beater, was acquitted. Black women responded that Simpson was on trial for murder, not abuse. The case, much like the Rodney King case, had exposed a racial fault line in American society—a deep divide between white and black. According to writer Jewelle Taylor Gibbs:

> Again, this society had to confront the reality that we inhabited one country geographically but were divided into two nations racially, culturally, economically, and politically.[35]

Chapter Six

The animated cast of the Simpsons, (from left to right) Marge, Maggie, Bart, Lisa, and Homer, became cultural icons of the 1990s as both adults and children enjoyed their often-cynical commentary on political and social life.

Pop Culture in the Digital Age

Music, movies, and the arts moved into the digital age in the 1990s. In the 1980s, most Americans turned to television for entertainment and information. But by 1998 TV faced strong competition from the Internet as more than 45 million people across the planet surfed the World Wide Web (WWW).

Choice was the watchword as Web surfers could buy their favorite album, book, or video right from their computer screen or browse home pages dedicated to their favorite artist. As the decade progressed, millions of companies large and small set up their own Web page or advertised in others. Internet ad revenue for 1997 was close to

$940 million, including on-line classifieds and directories.

The nineties saw the growth of megamedia corporations. The entertainment industry, for example, underwent waves of consolidation resulting in huge conglomerates capable of producing movies, books, videos, video games, music, TV programs, and magazines.

This consolidation caused a crossover in product promotion as never before. Local TV news shows promoted video releases, weekly news magazines put movie stars on their covers, and stone-faced network news anchors covered stories about the latest television sensation. Books and movies were created with an eye toward their suitability for packaging into sequels, cartoons, toys, and other spin-offs.

The most coveted consumers of media products were teenagers. There were almost 31 million teenagers in America in 1998, and their number was growing every year. Teens spent about $122 billion of their own and their parents' money each year, most of it on media-related products. Ninety percent of twelve to twenty-year-olds reported going to the movies frequently, and they purchased 26 percent of the movie tickets although they made up only 16 percent of the population. And at least 71 percent of teens bought full-length compact discs (CDs) at least once every three months.

The result was that entertainment and Internet-related businesses drove a huge segment of the American economy. And the boom was not confined to American shores. Movies, music, and related products became a huge source of foreign exports for the United States. In a truly worldwide phenomenon, people in China watched the feature film *Titanic*, people in South America danced to the music of Sheryl Crow, and people in over fifty countries tuned in to watch the series *Friends*.

TV in the 1990s

Two words describe the biggest television event of the nineties: Jerry Seinfeld. The sitcom *Seinfeld*, which began with a small viewership in 1989, became the most popular TV show of the decade. When it went off the air in 1998, the final episode was a huge media event with front-page coverage from newspapers and magazines and ongoing reportage from news and entertainment shows. Over 30 million people tuned in to watch the last *Seinfeld* episode.

More shows than ever were aimed at teenage viewers. According to a survey by Nielsen Media Research, excluding sports programs, the following

Is It News or Is It a Movie?

The gap between fact and fiction continued to shrink in the 1990s as TV newsmagazine shows blurred the lines between news and entertainment. An "infotainment" industry grew up to produce "docudramas"—TV shows based on real-life events. And it seemed the more violence or gossip involved, the higher the ratings. Viewers seemed to relate to average people who got into big trouble.

The story of Amy Fisher, a sixteen-year-old who shot her lover's middle-aged wife, became the subject of three made-for-TV movies, two of which were shown on the same night. This unleashed a flurry of similar movies. The made-for-TV movie of the case of Lyle and Erik Menendez, on trial for killing their parents, was shown before the trial was completed. The David Koresh/Branch Davidian tragedy became a movie within months of the actual event.

Blanket coverage was given to celebrities who committed crimes, as the ongoing O.J. Simpson saga proved. Other such events were the date rape allegations against William Kennedy Smith (nephew of Senator Edward Kennedy), child sex abuse charges against Michael Jackson, the assault on figure skater Nancy Kerrigan by rival skater Tonya Harding, and the scurrilous coverage of the presidential sex scandals.

shows were most watched by teens: *The Simpsons, King of the Hill, Seinfeld, Sabrina the Teenage Witch, Boy Meets World, Dawson's Creek, ER, Friends, Home Improvement,* and *Teen Angel.* Other popular shows among the young were *Buffy the Vampire Slayer,* and *Ally McBeal.*

The witty and sarcastic animated series *The Simpsons* was one of the premier comedies of the 1990s, and it helped shape and define the mildly cynical tone of the decade. The show became a wildly popular weekly series in the autumn of 1989. The result was a *Simpsons* merchandising explosion and a whopping viewership that gave credibility to the fledgling Fox Network.

The Simpsons spawned a series of cartoons aimed at an older audience. *Ren and Stimpy* appeared on cable's Nickelodeon channel. And a pair of famous low-life teenagers, *Beavis and Butt-head,* appeared on MTV. Just as viewers got used to the foul-mouthed humor of Beavis and Butt-head, along came the even raunchier *South Park* on Comedy Central. This was the first cartoon to have an MA-14 rating, not intended for viewers under fourteen.

Plugging into *Unplugged*

Television was popular, but music television was a hit. By 1990, MTV was seen in at least 50 million American homes. Advertisers flocked to MTV as the best way to reach millions of young consumers. Programmers at the music station continued to search for new ways to reach their young audience.

A show called *Unplugged* was a way to rebel against the slickness and prepackaged quality of some videos. On the show, artists played songs acoustically. *Unplugged* concerts featured some of the hottest acts in pop music, including rock icon Bob Dylan, New Jersey superstar Bruce Springsteen, Grammy winner Sheryl Crow, Irish pop group Cranberries, and the stunning grunge band Nirvana.

The Death of a Princess

On August 31, 1997, Diana, princess of Wales, died in a car accident when her drunk chauffeur hit a bridge post in a Paris tunnel at 100 miles per hour. Her driver was trying to escape the relentless paparazzi (photographers) who were trying to take pictures of the princess and her new boyfriend Dodi Fayed, who also died in the crash. The media had made the princess a larger-than-life celebrity, and Diana's death was one of the biggest media events of the decade.

The world mourned as television showed legions of Diana's admirers piling up flowers outside her London home or queuing for hours to sign one of the forty-three books of condolences in the apartments of Kensington Palace. At her funeral on September 6, mourners lined up twenty deep along the ten-mile route of her funeral procession.

Pallbearers carry Princess Diana's casket out of Westminster Abbey on September 6, 1997. Diana's death affected people around the world.

Pop star Elton John, a personal friend of Diana's, performed "Candle in the Wind '97," at her funeral. The song was a rewrite of a song John wrote in 1974 to honor Marilyn Monroe. When the CD was released on September 17, it became the fastest-selling single in history with 34 million sold. Proceeds were donated to some of Diana's favorite charities, via a newly established Diana, Princess of Wales, Memorial Fund.

Grunge and Alternative Music

Probably the biggest rock trend of the 1990s was grunge music, which incorporated elements of punk and heavy metal. Grunge first appeared in Seattle in 1990. Scores of musicians contributed to the movement, but three bands were pivotal in the rise of grunge: Nirvana, Pearl Jam, and Soundgarden.

In 1991 Nirvana released *Nevermind.* The driving beat and catchy melody made one track, "Smells Like Teen Spirit," the first anthem of grunge. The album eventually sold more than 7 million copies in the United States alone. By 1992 Nirvana was the first grunge band to make it onto the cover of the rock magazine *Rolling Stone.* Grunge fans were stunned on April 8, 1994, when Nirvana lead singer Kurt Cobain was found dead from a self-inflicted gunshot wound. Cobain's wife, Courtney Love, went on to achieve stardom with her band Hole.

Lead singer of Nirvana Kurt Cobain committed suicide in 1994. Cobain was a leader of a new rock sensation known as grunge rock.

In 1992 the rich, soaring vocals of the discontented Eddie Vedder helped sell 9 million copies of Pearl Jam's album *Ten.* In 1993 Pearl Jam made and broke records as their second album, *Vs.*, entered the national charts at number one, selling more than 950,000 copies the first week and setting a first-week-sales record.

Meanwhile, the grunge trend extended to clothing: Doc Marten or combat boots, ripped flannel, torn jeans, knit caps, mismatched stripes, and unkempt hair made it into a *Vogue* magazine fashion spread. Several big-name New York fashion designers adopted the look for their fashion shows.

Grunge continued its march into the mainstream after Cobain's death. Pearl Jam, now the main focus of the grunge movement, began to tour only sporadically, refused to make rock videos, and lowered its media profile. Its fourth album, *No Code,* was widely praised but sold a disappointing 1.3 million copies. By 1998 the band was still in a sales slump and grunge music was pronounced irrelevant by rock pundits.

Grunge evolved into alternative music, which had a more accessible, mainstream feel to it. Smashing Pumpkins was one band to achieve superstardom playing alternative rock. Its 1995 album *Mellon Collie and the Infinite Sadness,* sold more than 4 million copies.

Lollapalooza to Lilith

The success of alternative rock generated alternative rock festivals. The first

The Rock and Roll Hall of Fame

In 1995, rock and roll entered its middle age. It had come a long way since the 1950s. There was no better proof of that than the $92 million Rock and Roll Hall of Fame in Cleveland, Ohio. The impressive building, designed by architect I. M. Pei, features interactive exhibits (touch-screen computers that play requested songs and videos) and an array of music memorabilia. According to the September 4, 1995, *Time* magazine:

> The museum places heavy emphasis on rock's roots. One exhibit, called "The Beat Goes On," consists of several touch-screen computers showing video clips of rockers along with the performers who influenced them. Other exhibits are devoted to important rock precursors, such as blues greats Leadbelly and Howlin' Wolf. Here are plenty of intriguing curios on display as well—such as the Who drummer Keith Moon's grade school report card, saying he "is inclined to play the fool." There is flair in even the smallest detail: the building's ATMs look like jukeboxes.

The Rock Hall, as it is known, has inducted more than 150 artists to date. Each inductee has his or her own exhibit. Also displayed are such rare items as Jimi Hendrix's Fender Stratocaster guitar and the Beatles' handwritten lyrics. Innovations include a virtual jukebox that plays (on headphones) every song each inductee ever recorded. The Rock Hall draws over a million visitors a year to its 150,000-square-foot facility.

such festival was the multicultural Lollapalooza, which combined rap music, punk metal, and a wide variety of other musical styles. Lollapalooza was created in the summer of 1991 by Jane's Addiction singer Perry Farrell. No one thought that seven bands from seven clashing musical styles could prove successful, even if they did share alternative roots, but the festival worked.

The premier Lollapalooza tour was headlined by Ice-T's Body Count, English goth-rockers Siouxsie and the Banshees, black jazz-metal fusioneers Living Colour, punk-metal guitarist Henry Rollins, and scene-stealers Nine Inch Nails. The shows went smoothly, there were few culture clashes, and fans loved their newfound multicultural power. But by 1998 Farrell called it quits, announcing he couldn't find enough talent for another Lollapalooza.

In 1997 singer-songwriter Sarah McLachlan proved that women rock shows could draw huge crowds. McLachlan was frustrated that she could not get her music played on male-dominated radio stations. The singer defied conventional wisdom and began producing the all-female Lilith Fair, named after Adam's first wife of Hebrew legend. Despite industry warnings that an all-female roster would not sell tickets, Lilith grossed $16 million in thirty-eight shows, nearly doubling the take of the male-dominated Lollapalooza. A two-disc CD featuring live performances from Lilith grossed another $4 million.

Lilith featured a who's who of award-winning women rockers including Jewel, Paula Cole, Shawn Colvin, the Indigo Girls, Fiona Apple, Sheryl Crow, Suzanne Vega, Tracy Chapman, Bonnie Raitt, and Emmylou Harris. The 1998 Lilith Fair covered fifty-seven U.S. shows before it tested markets in Japan, Australia, and Europe.

For years, radio and record executives believed that there was limited demand for female artists and enforced informal signing quotas accordingly. They would offer contracts to dozens of male bands but perhaps only one female rocker per year. And radio stations limited the number of female artists on their playlists, almost never playing records by two women back to back. Indeed, concert promoters were reluctant to book the Lilith Fair, believing it would be unprofitable. Shawn Colvin states:

> We always knew that it wasn't true . . . that it was just sexist to think you couldn't have women on the same bill. It was just a matter of time before it would be proven false, and I'm only glad I was around when it happened. It's like an albatross being taken off your neck.[36]

In a 1990s phenomenon, female musical groups became extremely popular. Here, Sarah McLachlan (right) joins Heather Nova during Lilith Fair 1998. Lilith Fair featured all-female groups.

Lilith's success was helped by the fact that women became the largest purchasers of CDs, their share growing from 43 percent in 1988 to 51.4 percent in 1998. At the same time, many believed that women were producing some of the freshest music heard in years.

The Lilith Fair—which attracted 70 percent women, mostly ages seventeen to thirty-five—finally brought women back into the mainstream of music. The producers of Lilith donated $1 from every ticket to local charities.

Rap Tops the Charts

Women weren't the only group to change the face of nineties music. African Americans jumped to the top of record charts with the controversial urban sounds of hip-hop and rap music.

Dr. Dre (born Andre Young, 1965), former producer-rapper from the group N.W.A., started the trend in 1992 on the Death Row record label. His *The Chronic* went unexpectedly multiplatinum (over 2 million sold). Dre used the album as a springboard for other Death Row artists, including Snoop Doggy Dogg and the Dogg Pound.

The label, owned by Time-Warner, was later to find itself at the center of the 1995 media firestorm over responsibility for violent music releases like Dr. Dre's. Dre soon found himself doing five months in Pasadena City Jail for a parole violation after breaking a producer's jaw in 1992. He had several other prior assault offenses.

One of rap's biggest stars of the decade was Tupac Shakur. Under the name 2Pac, Shakur, twenty, recorded his first gold record, *2Pacalypse Now,* in 1991. Then–vice president Dan Quayle publicly claimed that the album's inflammatory lyrics about shooting police officers had influenced the killer of a Texas policeman.

As Shakur's career blossomed, his legal woes mounted. He was convicted of assault in 1992. In 1993 the rapper was picked up in New York and charged with sexual abuse of a female fan. On the day before the verdict was delivered in that case, three gunmen robbed Shakur at a midtown Manhattan studio of over $30,000 in jewelry and shot him four times. He appeared in court the next day in a wheelchair and was sentenced to one and a half to four and a half years for sexual abuse. While in jail, Shakur saw his *Me Against the World* reach number one on the Billboard charts.

On September 7, 1996, Shakur was in Las Vegas to watch a Mike Tyson boxing match. While sitting in the passenger seat of a BMW the rapper was shot four times by an unknown gunman. Shakur died from his injuries on September 13. Shortly after his death the video for "I Ain't Mad at Cha" was screened. Filmed a month before his death, it contained scenes of Tupac being shot and going to heaven, making it one of the most chilling artifacts of the rap era.

A Decade of Blockbuster Movies

Many successful American movies in the nineties featured compelling scripts or dazzling special effects. Steven Spielberg's *Jurassic Park* brought in huge box-office receipts with its astoundingly lifelike dinosaurs. Other special effects dazzlers included *The Addams Family, Batman, Independence Day, Titanic*, and *Armageddon.*

Jim Carrey was the highest-paid Hollywood star of the decade. His first six films, including *Ace Ventura: Pet Detective, Dumb and Dumber*, and *The Truman Show,* grossed over $667 million.

For *Liar Liar* the rubber-faced comedian was paid $20 million.

By the end of the 1990s, brash, bold young stars ruled the silver screen. A hot new crop of stars included Minnie Driver, Matthew McConaughey, Gwyneth Paltrow, Liv Tyler, Claire Danes, Ewan McGregor, Alicia Silverstone, Kate Winslet, and Leonardo DiCaprio.

DiCaprio became America's leading heartthrob in *Titanic*. The three-hour movie, directed by James Cameron, cost $200 million, but in 1997 and 1998 the film grossed a record $1 billion and won Academy Awards for best picture, best director, and nine other categories.

American films dominated the market but several foreign films gained wide acceptance in the United States. Among them were the Mexican film *Like Water for Chocolate*, the Irish suspense thriller *The Crying Game*, and the English comedy *The Full Monty*.

African Americans gained more power in Hollywood. Denzel Washington dazzled audiences in many movies, including *Malcolm X* and *Philadelphia*. Wesley Snipes proved his acting skill in Spike Lee's *Jungle Fever*, and Whoopi Goldberg won an Oscar for best supporting actress

Spike Lee

Director Spike Lee became well known in the 1990s for his controversial films that often highlighted the differences between blacks and whites.

Spike Lee, who focused his talents on dramatizing race relations with such movies as *Do the Right Thing*, remained the premier African American director in the 1990s. The commercial success of his films helped pave the way for other black directors, including the Hughes brothers and John Singleton. In 1992, Lee directed *Malcolm X*, a film biography of the slain civil rights leader. This led to massive sales of T-shirts and caps bearing the "X" logo from the movie. When the movie was released, Lee drew fire for saying that children should skip school to see the opening of *Malcolm X*. A 1996 film, *Get on the Bus*, about the Million Man March attracted critical acclaim, but was not well received at the box office.

in *Ghost.* Will Smith became one of the most popular movie stars for his roles in *Independence Day* and *Men in Black.*

Nineties Sports

Movies dominated the entertainment industry, but sports were a close second. The decade was marked by escalating player salaries, high prices for media rights, and misbehavior by athletes. Sports were extremely popular with fans. But several events dampened public enthusiasm and stripped away the ideal of innocent fun that sports had traditionally promoted. The first such event was the baseball strike.

Between 1984 and 1994, baseball had grown from a $600 million business to an industry worth almost $2 billion. On August 12, 1994, 750 members of the Major League Players Association went on strike. Never before had the games been halted so late in the season. Never before had the October play-offs and the World Series been canceled. When the strike was finally settled after 257 days, fans deserted their teams in droves, stadiums went half-filled, and TV broadcasts were unwatched. But by 1996, baseball's popularity once again began to climb.

After the baseball strike, players' escalating salaries became a hot topic. In 1997 the Atlanta Braves paid pitcher Greg Maddux $57.5 million for thirty-five starts a year (that is, $328,571 per game). Salaries were also hot in the National Basketball Association (NBA). In 1996 the Los Angeles Lakers agreed to pay Shaquille O'Neal $123 million over seven years. The Chicago Bulls paid Michael Jordan $30 million for his services in 1997 alone. Houston Rockets' pivotman Hakeem Olajuwon got $55 million for a five-year contract extension.

Fans were stunned when basketball star Kevin Garnett turned down a six-year, $103.5-million contract from the Minnesota Timberwolves because $209,349 per game wasn't enough money.

But it seemed the NBA could afford all the high-priced talent. In 1995 alone, the NBA took in $1.4 billion, excluding licensed merchandise, and its revenues were increasing by 15 percent a year.

As sports became more lucrative, teams held more sway over local politics. Cities were increasingly afraid of losing their major league teams to rival cities prepared to offer more attractive incentives. In 1995 alone, cities and states issued half a billion dollars' worth of bonds to build stadiums and arenas to keep or attract professional sports teams. Two teams moved out of Los Angeles that year, the Raiders to

Fans hold out signs that advertise their feelings about the impending baseball strike in 1994. The strike soured many fans on the sport, as it was hard to sympathize with players already making millions of dollars.

Oakland (attracted by $100 million in stadium renovations) and the Rams to St. Louis (which built a $270 million domed stadium as bait). Nashville lured the Houston Oilers with a proposed $290 million package.

Critics charged that the dollars spent on sports would be better spent on schools, libraries, road repair, and other civic problems or improvements. But the popularity of sports meant that the players and owners could keep on charging whatever the market would pay.

Interactive Pop Culture

Popular culture is by definition a reflection of the people who create and enjoy it. In the nineties, advanced communications allowed pop culture to become more interactive than ever before. Movies, sports, the Internet, fashion, and music all influenced each other in new and sometimes unexpected ways. Dennis Rodman alone was a movie star, an athlete, and a fashion statement who partied with rock stars.

Perhaps because the 1990s ended a millennium, culture became a kaleidoscopic reflection of all that had come before it. At the same time, culture looked forward to the twenty-first century, dabbling playfully with new technologies. In this way, pop culture reflected more diversity than ever before, and gave people the freedom to pick and choose from a broad landscape of entertainment and arts.

Chapter Seven

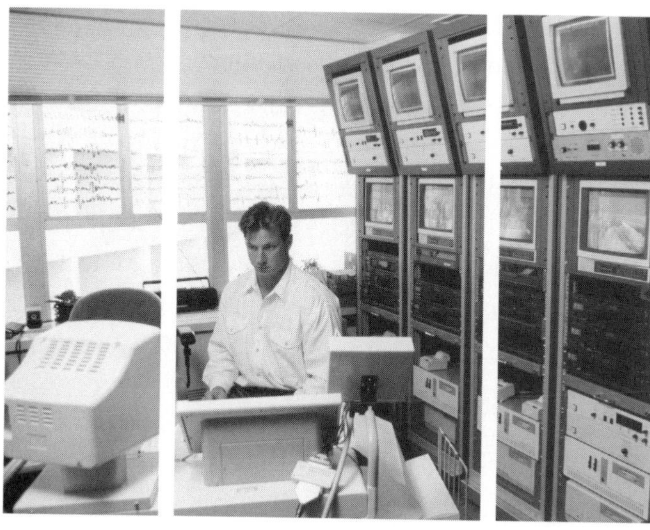

A computer technician works surrounded by high-tech equipment that became ever more common in the 1990s.

Technology, Medicine, and the Environment

The boundaries of technology, science, and medicine seemed practically unlimited in the last decade of the twentieth century. The capacity of computer memory continued to multiply and sophisticated silicon chips were found in everything from toys to VCRs to automobiles. Researchers cracked genetic codes and came closer than ever to conquering fatal diseases and solving the problems of infertility and old age.

Hundreds of communications satellites circled the earth performing tasks undreamed of a generation before. People received detailed directions and maps in their cars from global positioning system (GPS) devices. Palmtop computers allowed users to page people, send faxes, and even check e-mail from wherever they were standing. And healers in rural areas were able to communicate by computer with doctors in faraway cities to help the sick.

As the world neared the twenty-first century, the scientific wonders dreamed of decades ago simply became normal practices in everyday life.

Medical Miracles: Cancer

In the 1990s medical innovations came in a wide range of human afflictions including cancer, gene therapy, aging, strokes, AIDS, fertility, organ transplants, mental illnesses, and more.

Although cancer continued to kill about half a million people annually in the United States, research aimed at revealing the innermost secrets of cancer cells led to new ways to attack those cells. Although no magic bullet appeared to cure the complicated disease, a series of small improvements showed promise for pushing cancer death rates lower. Though doctors did not find a cure, they learned how to keep the disease at bay for months and sometimes years.

Doctors learned to combine therapeutic agents in an increasingly effective way as they came to believe that a single cure for cancer will never exist. In fact, doctors focused both on treating the disease and on preventing it. Research has shown that some types of cancer are preventable. Skin cancer, for example, is generally caused by repeated exposure to the sun's harmful rays. Lung cancer is usually caused by smoking, making it one of the most preventable cancers. Colon and rectal cancers may be prevented by eating fruits, whole grains, and vegetables.

Gene Therapy

DNA is the chemical blueprint of the human body. Coiled within its double helix are 3 billion chemical codes aggregated into genes, much like cities along an expressway. Genes determine the particular characteristics of a living creature, from weight and eye color to a genetic disposition to a disease.

One of the premier breakthroughs of the 1990s came in the field of gene therapy. Researchers continued to discover new genes and the role they played in disease. As a result, tests for the presence of genes that make people sick or make people susceptible to disease became more and more widely available. William Haseltime, chairman of a Maryland biotech firm, says,

> We are entering an era when disease will be predicted before it occurs. Medicine is basically going to change from treatment-based to a prevention-based discipline.[37]

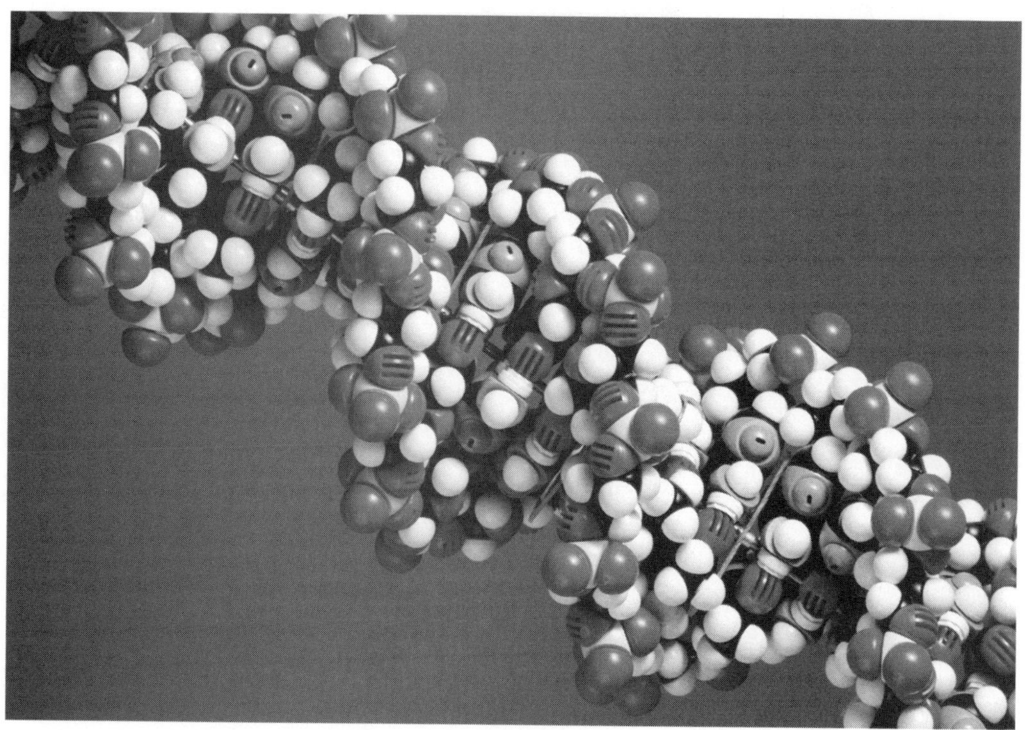

A model of the DNA helix. In the 1990s, scientists began work on the Human Genome Project, which aims to map and identify all of the fifty thousand to one hundred thousand genes in human DNA.

Seizing on the findings about disease genes and how they work, drug companies rushed to develop drugs that neutralize the effects of dangerous genes. Equally exciting, researchers in gene therapy were introducing genes into existing cells to prevent or cure a wide range of diseases, including cancer and AIDS. Gene therapists promised that within the next several decades, they will have identified a hundred or so genes that cause the most common diseases. Someday soon people will be able to order "genetic fingerprints" to predict their possible health history.

As the decade drew to a close, aided by money from the Human Genome Project, scientists were mapping and identifying all of the estimated fifty thousand to one hundred thousand human genes on human DNA. Their goal was to complete the study by 2005. Researchers were already making progress. As of 1997 they had identified more than six thousand human genes. Eleven of these

Who Wants to Know What's in Your Genes?

Genetic testing holds a promise of medical miracles. But it raised a host of ethical and legal questions in the 1990s. They were listed in *Time* magazine's special "Frontiers of Medicine" fall 1996 issue.

Could genetic testing be used by insurance companies or employers to identify those who might run up high insurance costs? Does genetic testing create an invasion of privacy, and would it stigmatize those who might have an inborn defect? Would prenatal testing lead to more abortions? Should anyone be tested before the age of eighteen?

Identifying disease was outpacing society's efforts to cope with the effects. Should someone with a family history of a fatal illness be told they have the "bad" gene and will die from it at a later time? "People have found that such testing is not as liberating as they thought," says one psychologist. "They end up hospitalized–not from the disease but for depression."

With widespread genetic testing in the near future, genetic counselors will be the fastest growing group of medical doctors. In 1998 only about one thousand genetic counselors offered a sophisticated understanding of both genetics and psychology. Explaining a patient's genetic test is very complicated and genetic counselors learn to do so without causing unnecessary anguish.

genes were disease genes, including one for breast cancer. The potential for genetic medicine seemed almost limitless. As Nobel Prize winner James Watson says, "We used to think that our fate was in the stars. Now we know that . . . our fate is in our genes."[38]

Making Babies

The first "test-tube" baby was conceived in England in 1978. The father's sperm and mother's egg were combined in a laboratory and the resulting embryo was later implanted in the mother's womb. This is called in vitro—literally, "in glass"—fertilization. Since that time, over thirty-three thousand babies have been conceived in vitro in the United States—seven thousand in 1994 alone. But in vitro fertilization is expensive, entails physical distress in the mother, and only works about 18 percent of the time.

However, in vitro technology has had an astounding effect on fertility research. Twenty years of manipulating embryos led researchers to solve problems in vitro alone could not solve. These techniques allowed people who are infertile, people with genetic disorders, people who have undergone cancer treatment, and older women to all have babies.

The numbers of people unable to conceive and/or bear children by natural methods rose during the 1990s. From 1988 to 1995 alone, the number of American women of childbearing age who suffered from fertility problems jumped from 4.9 million to 6.1 million, a 25 percent increase. The reasons for this trend are unclear but researchers point to a range of possibilities from delayed childbirth to environmental pollution.

The newest nineties techniques in assisted reproduction involved freezing a woman's eggs for later use. By this method, a woman who faced the loss of her egg-bearing ovaries through radiation therapy or disease could preserve her eggs in a laboratory. Younger women could freeze their eggs in the prime of life and use them later.

Egg freezing was just one of the fertility breakthroughs. Doctors were coaxing test-tube embryos to grow stronger before they were put into the womb and performing microscopic surgery to transfer chromosomes from old, worn-out eggs into young, robust ones.

These new techniques led to milestones in baby making and to debates about the ethics of such procedures. In 1994 a sixty-two-year-old Italian woman gave birth to a child conceived via a donated egg and her husband's sperm. Her case prompted a moral debate as to whether an elderly woman could properly care for an infant.

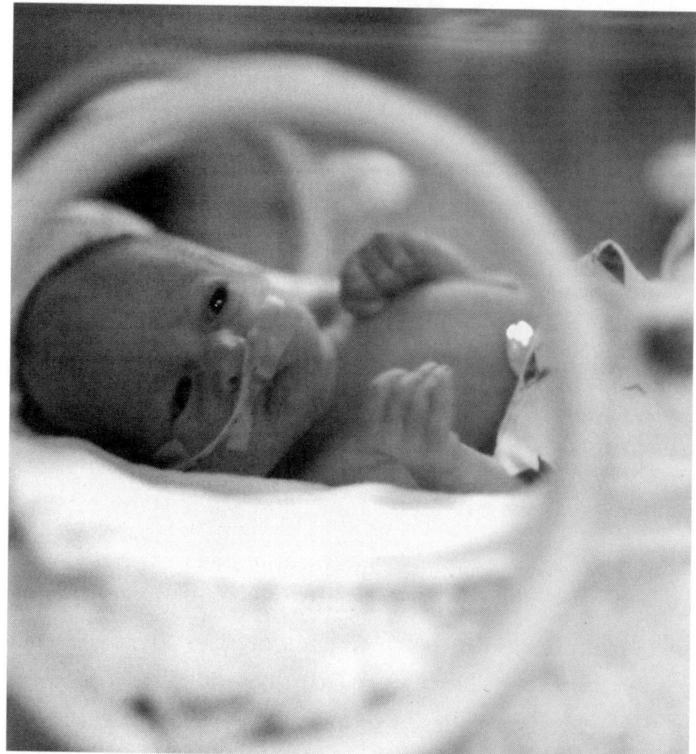

Kenneth McCaughey is one of the septuplets born to Bobbi and Kenny McCaughey after the couple used fertility drugs to conceive.

Cloning

The first genetically reproduced sheep, Dolly, led to controversy in the scientific community. Some heralded the experiment while others predicted that it would lead to bizarre experiments in human reproduction.

In 1997 researchers in Edinburgh, Scotland, created a lamb named Dolly from a single cell of an adult sheep. This practice, called cloning, was a major advance in reproduction technology. But it was startling as well. Unlike normal offspring, Dolly was an exact copy of her mother—her identical twin.

Once the cloning method is refined, most skilled laboratory technicians should be able to reproduce the results. This frightened people. Although the cloners struggled for ten years to cross that biological barrier, it was a matter of days before religious and political leaders spoke out against the practice. If scientists can clone sheep, they argued, they might soon be able to clone humans.

Cloning could become a useful tool. Farmers could clone their prize-winning cows to produce more milk from smaller herds. Sheep ranchers could do the same with top lamb and wool producers. Cloning could also be useful in medicine for use in regeneration of damaged spinal cords, heart muscles, and brain tissues.

But the press wasted no time in imagining far more fantastic uses of cloning: virgin births, resurrection of the dead (including armies of Hitlers or Husseins), or women giving birth to themselves. One biologist quipped on the front page of the *New York Times* that if cloning were perfected "there'd be no need for men." But scientists were still a long way from cloning humans, at least for the time being.

Technology Saving Lives

Computers revolutionized many aspects of life in the 1990s, including medicine, helping to save time and money as well as people's lives. In the 1970s, heart doctors basically guessed what caused heart attacks. In the 1990s, doctors were able to use nuclear imaging and huge computer databases to treat heart attacks with astonishing efficiency.

One such database is the Medical Center Databank for Cardiovascular

Disease at Duke University. Recorded on its silicon chips are details of thousands of heart attacks over nearly thirty years. Each heart spasm, each dying heart muscle, each patient's treatment is registered and analyzed by the computer. Worldwide, doctors on five continents can dial into the system, type in a patient's symptoms, and get a recommended treatment based on thousands of patients who have had similar problems. Besides saving lives, the machine tells doctors when patients may safely be released to go home, which saves hospitals money.

Motivated to save time, money, and lives, and earn profits by doing so, hundreds of medical technology firms were created to develop new and better machines. Computers like the one at Duke help doctors treat a wide range of diseases. Doctors punch in details of a patient's condition—or wire the patient directly to the computer—then wait for answers. Called POEMS (Post Operative Expert Medical System), the machines help less experienced doctors treat patients even in remote corners of the globe.

POEMS have allowed a new form of treatment called telemedicine. Medical experts can "visit" patients via the telephone, not to talk, but to analyze their conditions through telemedical links at small clinics. In this manner, highly skilled doctors can share their expertise with doctors hundreds or thousands of miles away.

The idea of transferring knowledge instead of patients may be the most important medical trend of the decade. As the world became more and more "wired," knowledge once disseminated over weeks, months, or years moved in a matter of minutes. In a profession where seconds can mean the difference between life and death, the new machines were saving almost as many lives as modern miracle drugs.

It's a Wired World

While computers were helping heal millions of people, most Americans used their desktop personal computers (PCs) for less important matters. By 1998 more than 45 million people were wired into the World Wide Web (WWW), allowing them to pursue interests from shopping to touring art museums to listening to their favorite band, all without leaving home. The explosive growth of the Web was primarily a 1990s phenomenon (the Internet itself was mainly developed during the 1980s).

The point-and-click graphics and text of the World Wide Web emerged in 1994 and 1995. The ground rules for the Web were first developed by Tim Berners-Lee for astronomers at Switzer-

An Internet user browses the Web in a nationwide pastime. The World Wide Web gave people access to an almost unlimited amount of information.

land's CERN (the European Laboratory for Particle Physics) between 1989 and 1992. The Web was originally used by scientists who needed to exchange photos and illustrations along with text.

The practically limitless potential of the Web was first noticed by big business in August 1995 when Netscape, the leading provider of Web-browsing software, went public: Its first stock offering made twenty-four year-old cofounder Marc Andreesen $50 million richer overnight.

As the year 2000 drew near, the Web revolution was still in its infancy. Users experienced delays in connections, slow downloads, and limited ability to utilize sound and moving pictures. This was beginning to change as the programming language of the Web evolved to incorporate multimedia enhancements and a new generation of cable and phone lines allowed faster downloading.

Cars of the 1990s

While computers and the Internet taught and entertained, the main

The Year 2000 Bug

There is a possibility that the entire computer revolution could come crashing to a halt at midnight on December 31, 1999. That's when the internal clocks of millions of computerized devices will flip from the abbreviated year "99" to "00." That bit of shorthand is how most programmers of years past, intent on saving memory space when it was thousands of times costlier than today, designated the year. Many computers go into the equivalent of shock when they read a year date of 00, thinking it is 1900. The machines and devices they drive stop, print out wrong information, or otherwise malfunction.

This problem is variously called the "millennium bug," the "year 2000 problem," or simply the "Y2K bug." It has created the biggest dilemma of the computer age and a billion-dollar growth industry to fix it. Failure to deal with the problem could cause telephones and lights to go dead and factories to shut down, possibly pushing the world into a serious recession.

The cost of fixing the Y2K bug could reach $300 to $600 billion. And those numbers are dwarfed by the $1 trillion the federal government is spending to fix computers that oversee the Internal Revenue Service, the Social Security Administration, federal banks, and dozens of other institutions. Some doomsday scenarios for the Y2K bug include wiping out millions of bank balances; shutting down nuclear power plants, causing meltdowns; and even launching nuclear missiles when military computers shut down.

As of this writing, no one is sure exactly what will happen in the year 2000 when the world's computers become confused and think it is the year 1900.

American machine remained the automobile. In past decades, the focus of car design was on style and speed. But in the 1990s, as millions of cars clogged the highways, consumers were more interested in safety and quality.

As the decade began, America's big three automakers—Chrysler, General Motors (GM), and Ford—were falling behind in the marketplace. The best-selling car in America was the Honda Accord, followed by the Toyota Camry. After GM lost $11.7 billion in 1992, it launched a new car called the Saturn, built by the first new American car company in thirty years.

By 1993, the big three began to lease cars in addition to selling them. With leasing programs consumers could afford to drive more expensive vehicles than they could purchase outright. As the price of cars rose to an average of $22,000, people began to purchase less expensive trucks. Sales of pickups soared and by the end of the decade, the Ford F-series pickup was the best-selling American vehicle followed by the Chevrolet C-series.

Americans didn't often use their trucks for work, but they did use them for play. In the early '90s, four-wheel-drive vehicles like the Ford Explorer, the Chevy Blazer, and the Jeep Grand Cherokee dominated the sport utility vehicle (SUV) market. Foreign automakers jumped on the SUV bandwagon, and by the end of the nineties, the large vehicles came in all shapes and sizes from the Toyota RAV to the Mercedes Benz M320.

For those who liked their cars swift, sleek, and low to the ground, 1997 saw the introduction of some uniquely designed sports cars. The Plymouth Prowler looked like a modernized high-tech race car with classic lines. The $67,000 Dodge Viper GTS resembled something out of a science-fiction movie.

While trucks, sports cars, and SUVs guzzled plenty of gas, car makers realized that oil will be in short supply by the middle of the next decade. To solve that problem, General Motors introduced the first production electrical vehicle, the EV1, in 1997. The car had a range of seventy miles and could be recharged in two to three hours.

As the decade drew to a close, all the world's car makers were working on prototypes of "green machines"—non-oil-burning vehicles. Some ran on electricity, others on the hydrogen molecules in water, others on a combination of gas, electricity, and hydrogen.

Earth and the Environment in the 1990s

In spite of their driving habits, polls revealed that a majority of Americans continued to be concerned about the environment.

On April 22, 1990, Earth Day celebrated its twentieth anniversary, claiming 200 million participants worldwide who gathered together to celebrate the ecology movement. (The first Earth Day was held in 1970 with 20 million participants; many credit this event with launching the modern environmental movement.) Throughout the nineties, Americans concerned about the environment continued to celebrate Earth Day. But humankind's effects on the earth continued to cause environmental problems.

Denis Hayes who helped organize the first Earth Day and the 20th Anniversary Earth Day in 1990, said: "The world is in worse shape today than it was 20 years ago."[39] While this opinion may be debated by experts, a 1994 Gallup poll showed that 75 percent of those surveyed expressed concern about environmental problems. Eighty-two percent supported strict laws to protect the environment. Sixty-seven percent said they would pay higher costs for en-

A man waves an earth flag on the twentieth anniversary of the first Earth Day held in Washington, D.C. The state of the environment remained a cause for public concern in the 1990s.

vironmental protection. Nearly 75 percent said there should be increased regulations to protect water, 66 percent wanted more protection against air pollution, and over half replied that wildlife areas, wetlands, and endangered species needed more protection.

These concerns prompted an Earth Summit in Rio de Janeiro in 1992. Over one hundred heads of state met to find ways to solve environmental problems. In 1997 they met again at Earth Summit+5. One of the commitments made at the second Earth Summit was to reduce car-related carbon-dioxide emissions which are believed to cause global warming. Wealthy industrialized countries agreed that by 2000 their emissions of climate-changing greenhouse gases, particularly carbon dioxide, would be no higher than in 1990. But as the decade ended, only Great Britain, Switzerland, Holland, and Germany were able to live up to the modest agreement.

The Earth Summits had mixed results. While deforestation, overfishing, greenhouse emissions, species extinction, and the water supply all worsened after 1992, water quality improved, and so did health and life expectancy. Emissions of lead, soot, and chlorofluorocarbons were down.

Although environmental concerns became a very public and divergent issue in the 1990s, many problems remained unresolved.

Epilogue

The Manhattan skyline in New York City reveals the high-tech, modern look of many cities. As the 1990s ended, many people wondered what the future would bring.

Into the Twenty-First Century

The year 2000 represents the end of a decade, the end of the twentieth century, and the end of the second millennium. The average American's daily life utilized thousands of brilliant ideas that were gathered slowly over centuries, gathered speed in the twentieth century, then snowballed in the 1990s. A one-hundred-year-old person in 1999 could remember a time when cars, airplanes, radio, television, nuclear bombs, computers, and the Internet did not exist.

The 1990s will be remembered as a time of relative peace, when the economy was booming, medical miracles were in the daily news, and America became an interactive, Net-surfing nation. But what of the years that lie ahead?

Growing Population

In 1900, the world's population was just over 1 billion people—fewer than the number of people who live in China today. Although great wars tarnished the twentieth century, killing hundreds of millions of people, by the year 2000, the world's population will reach well over 6 billion. By the year 2020, it is projected that there will be 7.5 to 8.5 billion people—nearly 50 percent more people than live on the planet today.

Ninety-three percent of the population growth will occur in developing countries. Sixty percent of the world will live in cities. Scientists project that a population that has increased by half in twenty-five years may require 75 percent more food and fiber and 100 percent more energy. And researchers at Johns Hopkins University predict that by 2025, the world may be incapable of feeding its estimated 8 billion inhabitants. (These predictions are difficult to confirm. New technologies may be able to feed an extra 2 billion people. In 1998 alone, some 18 million people starved around the world—but it was usually politics, not agricultural limitations, that killed them.)

These 8 billion people will be closely connected in many ways. Instant communications will spread to the far corners of the globe. Borders of countries will mean less as cooperation on economic grounds becomes even more important than it is today. However, such connectedness will not necessarily make everyone alike. Strong currents of ethnic, national, and religious conflict may emerge.

Many researchers believe that humanity cannot avoid massive environmental change. Global climatic changes in precipitation, cloudiness, humidity, sea level, weather extremes, and other aspects of the environment will add to human-induced changes. These changes have already begun.

The shared resources of the Internet may help ease pressure on the earth. Researchers in countries across the planet are already studying ways to accommodate the growing population. A global move toward sustainable development is taking place. This means figuring out ways to use nature's bounty efficiently, so that necessary resources and critical life support systems will be available for future generations.

For sustainable development to occur, a new agricultural and industrial revolution will be needed. This movement will increase efficiency and minimize waste. And there will be many born in the twenty-first century who will work together to help humankind tackle these problems.

A crowded street in Beijing, China. Will a population boom bring problems as the new millennium breaks?

Back to the Future

No one can predict exactly what will happen in the next century. If trends continue, life may become even easier for those who live in industrial countries. New technologies will continue to cure disease and churn out high-tech electric goods such as cell phones, digital recorders, and even home-based virtual reality. As the country fills up with a larger population, people might opt to stay at home much of the time. Following current trends, they will "go to work" on their computers, order videos and record albums over the Internet, and have their food delivered to their homes.

More people are living past the age of one hundred than ever before. And it's a safe bet that a one-hundred-year-old living in the year 2090 will scarcely recognize the world in which he or she was born into way back in 1990—the good old days.

Notes

Chapter One: Big Changes in Washington

1. Quoted in Associated Press Writers, *Twentieth Century America,* vol. 10, *An Uneasy Peace: 1988–*. New York: Grolier, 1995, p. 137.
2. Quoted in Associated Press Writers, *An Uneasy Peace: 1988–*, p. 145.
3. Quoted in Associated Press Writers, *An Uneasy Peace: 1988–*, p. 154.
4. Lance Morrow, "Newt's World," *Time*, December 25, 1995–January 1, 1996, p. 80.

Chapter Two: The Post–Cold War World

5. Quoted in Larry Berman and Emily O. Goldman, *The Clinton Presidency.* Chatham, NJ: Chatham House Publishers, 1996, p. 290.
6. Zlatko Dizadarevic, *Sarajevo: A War Journal.* New York: Fromm International, 1993, p. xvi.
7. Dizadarevic, *Sarajevo*, p. 40.
8. Quoted in Associated Press Writers, *An Uneasy Peace: 1988–*, p. 52.
9. Quoted in Associated Press Writers, *An Uneasy Peace: 1988–*, p. 53.
10. Quoted in Associated Press Writers, *An Uneasy Peace: 1988–*, p. 53.
11. Quoted in Associated Press Writers, *An Uneasy Peace: 1988–*, p. 61.

Chapter Three: Violence in America

12. Quoted in Richard Lacayo, "Cult of Death," *Time*, March 15, 1993, p. 36.
13. Quoted in Associated Press Writers, *An Uneasy Peace: 1988–*, pp. 86–87.
14. Quoted in Nicholas Kenney, "Klan Power Wanes; Hate, Bigotry Edge Toward the Militias," *National Catholic Reporter*, October 25, 1996, p. 3.
15. Quoted in Lance Williams and Scott Winokur, "Militia Extremists Defend Their Views," *San Francisco Examiner*, April 25, 1995.
16. Quoted in David E. Kaplan and Mike Tharp, "Terrorism Threats at Home: Two Years After Oklahoma City, Violent Sects Abound," *U.S. News & World Report*, December 29, 1997, p. 22.
17. Quoted in Alexander Cockburn, "Land of the Free," *New Statesman & Society,* October 1, 1995, p. 14.

Chapter Four: Trends in Family and Education

18. Quoted in Pat Wingert, "Teen Pregnancy," *Newsweek*, April

11, 1998, p. 40.

19. Quoted in Wingert, "Teen Pregnancy," p. 41.
20. Quoted in Gini Holland, *America in the 20th Century, 1990s*. New York: Marshall Cavendish, 1995, p. 1,357.
21. Quoted in Andrea Atkins and Jeremy Schlosberg, "Dressed to Learn: Are Schools Better . . . When Kids Are in Uniform?" *Better Homes and Gardens*, August 1996, p. 42.
22. Quoted in Atkins and Schlosberg, "Dressed to Learn," p. 42.
23. Quoted in David Brauer and John McCormick, "The Boys Behind the Ambush," *Newsweek*, April 6, 1998.
24. Quoted in Geoffrey Cowley, "Why Children Turn Violent," *Newsweek*, April 6, 1998, p. 20.
25. Margot Hornblower, "Great Xpectations," *Time*, June 9, 1997, p. 28.
26. Quoted in Hornblower, "Great Xpectations," p. 61.

Chapter Five: Gender and Race Conflict

27. Quoted in Jewelle Taylor Gibbs, *Race and Justice*. San Francisco: Jossey-Bass, 1996, p. 31.
28. Quoted in Gibbs, *Race and Justice*, p. 28.
29. Quoted in Gibbs, *Race and Justice*, p. 42.
30. Quoted in Associated Press Writers, *An Uneasy Peace: 1988–*, p. 73.
31. Quoted in Gibbs, *Race and Justice*, p. 55.
32. Quoted in Gibbs, *Race and Justice*, p. 56.
33. Quoted in Mary Hull, *Struggle and Love*. Philadelphia: Chelsea House, 1997, p. 97.
34. Quoted in Gibbs, *Race and Justice*, p. 130.
35. Gibbs, *Race and Justice*, p. 217.

Chapter Six: Pop Culture in the Digital Age

36. Quoted in Robert Hillburn, "They Said She Couldn't Do It," *Los Angeles Times*, June 21, 1998, Sunday Calender section, p. 4.

Chapter Seven: Technology, Medicine, and the Environment

37. Quoted in J. Madeline Nash, "The Enemy Within," *Time*, Special Issue, "The Frontiers of Medicine," Fall 1996, p. 25.
38. Quoted in Nash, "The Enemy Within," p. 25.
39. Quoted in Timothy O'Riordan, William C. Clark et al., "The Legacy of Earth Day: Reflections at a Turning Point," *Environment*, April 1995, p. 6.

Chronology

1990

February 4: Mass rallies and strikes are held to protest Communist rule in the Soviet Union.

August 2: Iraq invades Kuwait and the United States initiates Operation Desert Shield.

August 16: U.S. soldiers arrive in Saudi Arabia as part of Operation Desert Shield.

October: President George Bush reneges on his campaign pledge and raises taxes.

1991

January 16: Coalition airplanes begin massive bombing raids on Iraq to begin Operation Desert Storm.

February 28: The Gulf War officially ends.

June 6: Boris Yeltsin is elected president of the Russian Republic.

August 19: Soviet general secretary Mikhail Gorbachev is briefly deposed by Communist hard-liners in a failed coup.

August 29: The Soviet legislature suspends all activities of the Communist Party, the first time in seventy years that the USSR is not ruled by Communists.

October 15: Clarence Thomas is confirmed as a justice of the U.S. Supreme Court.

December 25: Gorbachev resigns and transfers power to Yeltsin; the Soviet Union is dissolved and replaced by a Commonwealth of Independent States.

1992

April 29: The not guilty verdict in the Rodney King case ignites riots in Los Angeles.

June 28: The most severe earthquake in forty years, measuring 7.4 on the Richter scale, rocks the Yucca Valley in California; one child is killed, 350 are injured.

August: Ethnic cleansing begins in Bosnia-Herzegovina as Serb nationalists begin a campaign of terror and genocide against Muslims.

August 21: Federal agents engage Randall Weaver, his family, and a friend, in a shootout at Ruby Ridge, Idaho, killing Weaver's fourteen-year-old son, Samuel, and his wife, Vicki.

November 2: Bill Clinton, with running mate Al Gore, wins the national presidential race.

December 9: U.S. troops land in Somalia to deliver humanitarian aid.

1993

February 11: Janet Reno is appointed the first female attorney general of the United States.

February 26: The World Trade Center in New York City is bombed.

February 28: The ATF attempts to serve a warrant on the Branch Davidian compound in Waco, Texas; the resulting shootout kills four federal agents and wounds sixteen, while six Branch Davidians are killed.

April 19: The standoff with the Branch Davidians ends with a firestorm that kills more than eighty people.

1994

January: The Justice Department subpoenas files pertaining to the Clintons' Whitewater investments, starting an investigation that would last more than four years.

January 17: A major earthquake measuring 6.6 on the Richter scale hits Los Angeles, killing fifty-five people.

February: NATO begins its first offensive in Bosnia when U.S. jet fighters shoot down four Serbian jets.

September 27: Hundreds of Republican candidates gather on the steps of the Capitol building to sign the Contract with America.

November 8: In midterm elections, Republicans gain a majority in the House and Senate for the first time in over forty years.

1995

April 19: The Alfred P. Murrah Federal Building in Oklahoma City is bombed, killing 168.

September: The *New York Times* and the *Washington Post* jointly print the Unabomber's manifesto.

December 14: The presidents of Bosnia, Croatia, and Serbia sign a peace accord in Paris.

1996

August 22: Clinton signs the Personal Responsibility and Work Opportunity Act, which changes welfare rules for 13 million Americans.

November: Clinton becomes the first Democrat to be reelected as president since 1944; the Republican Congress is first to be elected since 1930.

1997

Clinton announces a plan to link every U.S. classroom to the Internet by the year 2000.

April: Researchers in Scotland clone a lamb named Dolly from a single cell of an adult sheep.

June 2: Timothy McVeigh is convicted on eleven counts of murder and conspiracy in relation to the Oklahoma City bombing; he is sentenced to die by lethal injection.

Summer: The Lilith Fair grosses $16 million in thirty-eight shows with an all-female roster of rock musicians.

August 31: Diana, princess of Wales, dies in a car accident in a Paris tunnel.

October 2: Luke Woodham, sixteen, kills his mother and, in a gruesome trend of schoolyard killings, kills two classmates and wounds seven.

1998

May: Theodore J. Kaczynski, also known as the Unabomber, is given four life sentences plus thirty years in prison for killing three people and injuring twenty-nine with his homemade mail bombs.

For Further Reading

Associated Press Writers, *Twentieth Century America*. Vol. 10, *An Uneasy Peace: 1988–*. New York: Grolier, 1995. A history of the Bush era and the 1992 election, taken directly from Associated Press reports written as the news was unfolding.

Zlatko Dizadarevic, *Sarajevo: A War Journal*. New York: Fromm International, 1993. A diary, written with dignity, irony, and even humor, of the destruction of Sarajevo.

Kathlyn Gay, *Saving the Environment: Debating the Costs*. New York: Franklin Watts, 1996. A book that looks at both sides of the environmental debate with detailed facts about problems and solutions.

Jewelle Taylor Gibbs, *Race and Justice*. San Francisco: Jossey-Bass, 1996. This book covers the Rodney King beating, the LA riots, and the O.J. Simpson trial in great detail. Good analysis of racial and gender conflicts that swirled around those events.

Mary Hull, *Struggle and Love*. Philadelphia: Chelsea House, 1997. A book for young adults about African American history from 1972 to 1997.

Tom McGrath, *MTV: The Making of a Revolution*. Philadelphia: Running Press, 1996. An oversized book that covers the rise of MTV in detail.

Fred Whitehead, ed., *Culture Wars*. San Diego: Greenhaven Press, 1994. A book that debates diverse current issues in American culture, from teaching the classics to Madonna and rock music.

Works Consulted

Andrea Atkins and Jeremy Schlosberg, "Dressed to Learn: Are Schools Better . . . When Kids Are in Uniform?" *Better Homes and Gardens*, August 1996. An article about the pros and cons of student uniforms.

Larry Berman and Emily O. Goldman, *The Clinton Presidency.* Chatham, NJ: Chatham House Publishers, 1996. A technical analysis of the Clinton administration's first term.

David Brauer and John McCormick, "The Boys Behind the Ambush," *Newsweek*, April 6, 1998. An article about the schoolyard killings in Jonesboro, Arkansas, that tells about the boys who committed the crime.

Alexander Cockburn, "Land of the Free," *New Statesman & Society,* October 1, 1995. This is a long article discussing the philosophy of the Unabomber as detailed in Kaczynski's manifesto printed in the *New York Times* and the *Washington Post* in 1995.

Geoffrey Cowley, "Why Children Turn Violent," *Newsweek*, April 6, 1998. From the *Newsweek* cover story about the shootings in Jonesboro, Arkansas.

Robert Hillburn, "They Said She Couldn't Do It," *Los Angeles Times,* June 21, 1998. From an article in the Sunday Entertainment section about Sarah McLachlan and her success as the founder of the Lilith Fair.

Gini Holland, *America in the 20th Century, 1990s*. New York: Marshall Cavendish, 1995. A big, easy-to-read book about all aspects of American culture from 1990 to 1995.

Lars B. Johanson, ed., *Statistical Abstract of the United States*. Washington, DC: Government Printing Office, 1996. An annual publication of the U.S. Bureau of Census that tallies detailed statistics about all aspects of American life including population, travel, employment, food prices, natural resources, trade, and more.

David E. Kaplan and Mike Tharp, "Terrorism Threats at Home: Two Years After Oklahoma City, Violent Sects Abound," *U.S. News & World Report*, December 29, 1997. An article from an issue dedicated to the rising militia movement and how the government is combating the increasing threats.

Nicholas Kenney, "Klan Power Wanes; Hate, Bigotry Edge Toward the Militias," *National Catholic Reporter*, October 25, 1996. An article detailing the loss of power within the Ku Klux Klan and how its ideology of racist, anti-Semitic, and violent views have been picked up by some militia movements.

Richard Lacayo, "Cult of Death," *Time*, March 15, 1993. An article written about David Koresh and his followers immediately after the compound was destroyed.

Los Angeles Times, Understanding the Riots: Los Angeles Before and after the Rodney King Case. Los Angeles: *Los Angeles Times*, 1992. A day-by-day account of the 1965 Watts riots and the 1992 LA uprising and its aftermath. Taken from the pages of the *LA Times* and full of often-unpleasant, full-page, color photographs.

Michael Moore, *Downsize This!* New York: Crown, 1996. A hilarious book by the maker of the 1989 film *Roger and Me*. Full of populist humor and outrageous shenanigans aimed at corporate America.

Lance Morrow, "Newt's World," *Time*, December 25, 1995–January 1, 1996. This magazine features Newt Gingrich as *Time* magazine's 1995 Man of the Year. The article covers Gingrich's rise to power from a liberal Republican to a conservative Speaker of the House.

J. Madeline Nash, "The Enemy Within," *Time*, Special Issue, "The Frontiers of Medicine," Fall 1996. An article about medical discoveries in a special issue of *Time* dedicated to health and modern medical miracles.

Timothy O'Riordan, William C. Clark, Robert W. Kates, and Alan McGowan, "The Legacy of Earth Day: Reflections at a Turning Point," *Environment*, April 1995. From an article detailing the good and bad things that have happened to the environment since the first Earth Day in 1970.

Time-Warner's Pathfinder Network. This website ties into thousands of articles that have appeared in *Time, Life, People, Fortune, Entertainment Weekly*, and other sources. An extremely valuable tool for finding out about recent news events and cultural stories. Available at http://www.pathfinder.com/search/altavista/index.html.

Lance Williams and Scott Winokur, "Militia Extremists Defend Their Views," *San Francisco Examiner*, April 25, 1995. An article from San Francisco's daily paper that details the rise of the milita movement particularly in California.

Pat Wingert, "Teen Pregnancy," *Newsweek*, April 11, 1998. From a short article about the drop in teenage pregnancy rates.

Index

Picture Credits

Cover photos, (from left to right): Reuters/Corbis-Bettmann, Bettmann, Archive Photos/20th Century Fox
Mark E. Ahlstrom, 62
Agence France Presse/Corbis-Bettmann, 51
AP Wide World Photos, 6, 14, 76, 89, 93, 109
Archive Photos, 86
Archive Photos/AMW Pressedienst GMBH, 106
Archive Photos/Fotos International, 83
Archive Photos/Saga, 95
CNP/Archive Photos, 53
Library of Congress, 20
© 1991 Arnie Sachs/Consolidated News Pictures/Archive Photos, 74 (right)
© 1991 Ron Sachs/Consolidated News Pictures/Archive Photos, 13
© 1993 Ron Sachs/Consolidated News Pictures/Archive Photos, 18
PhotoDisc, 59, 60, 64, 99, 101, 110
Reuters/Peter Andrews/Archive Photos, 33
Reuters/Archive Photos, 39
Reuters/Pat Benic/Archive Photos, 36
Reuters/Blank Children's Hospital/Archive Photos, 103
Reuters/Mark Cardwell/Archive Photos, 47
Reuters/Lee Celano/Archive Photos, 90
Reuters/Corbis-Bettmann, 11, 22, 27, 29, 72, 78, 81, 97
Reuters/Milos Cvetkovic/Archive Photos, 32
Reuters/Richard Ellis/Archive Photos, 42
Reuters/Gary Hershorn/Archive Photos, 12
Reuters/Ho/Archive Photos, 46
Reuters/John Kuntz/Archive Photos, 68
Reuters/Kimimasa Mayama/Archive Photos, 23
Reuters/Win McNamee/Archive Photos, 15, 40
Reuters/Eric Miller/Archive Photos, 55
Reuters/Sam Mircovich/Archive Photos, 80, 85
Reuters/Jeff Mitchell/Archive Photos, 44, 49, 50, 104
Reuters/Dennis Owen/Archive Photos, 112
Reuters/Pool/Archive Photos, 34, 69
Reuters/Blake Sell/Archive Photos, 24
Reuters/John Sommers II/Archive Photos, 67
Reuters/Mike Theiler/Archive Photos, 45
Reuters/Thomas/Archive Photos, 82
Reuters/Rick Wilking/Archive Photos, 74 (left)
UPI Corbis-Bettmann, 7, 8

About the Author

Stuart A. Kallen is the author of more than 125 nonfiction books for children and young adults. He has written on topics ranging from Soviet history to rock and roll to the space shuttle. Mr. Kallen lives in San Diego, California.